T0213722

SpringerBriefs in Computer Science

More information about this series at http://www.springer.com/series/10028

Ilaiah Kavati · Munaga V.N.K. Prasad
Chakravarthy Bhagvati

Efficient Biometric Indexing and Retrieval Techniques for Large-Scale Systems

 Springer

Ilaiah Kavati
MLR Institute of Technology
Hyderabad, Andhra Pradesh
India

Chakravarthy Bhagvati
University of Hyderabad
Hyderabad, Andhra Pradesh
India

Munaga V.N.K. Prasad
Institute for Development and Research
   in Banking Technology
Hyderabad, Andhra Pradesh
India

ISSN 2191-5768   ISSN 2191-5776   (electronic)
SpringerBriefs in Computer Science
ISBN 978-3-319-57659-6   ISBN 978-3-319-57660-2   (eBook)
DOI 10.1007/978-3-319-57660-2

Library of Congress Control Number: 2017939089

Printed on acid-free paper

This Springer imprint is published by Springer Nature
The registered company is Springer International Publishing AG
The registered company address is: Gewerbestrasse 11, 6330 Cham, Switzerland

To My Family and Teachers

Preface

In our daily life, we use certain characteristics of people such as facial features, voice, gait, etc., to recognize people who are familiar to us. Automatic identification of the people by the use of their physiological (such as face, fingerprint, iris, hand geometry, etc.) and/or behavioral (such as voice, signature, gait, etc.) characteristics is called biometrics. As biometric characteristics are distinctive, cannot be forgotten or lost, and the person to be authenticated needs to be physically present at the point of access, biometric-based identification systems are gaining popularity and deployed in many important applications. In biometric identification systems, the identity corresponding to a query image is determined by sequentially matching it against all enrolled images in the database. Typically this approach works well for small databases. However, in real-life scenarios, size of biometric databases are usually high (e.g., Unique Identification Authority of India) and this sequential search makes the identification process extremely slow and computationally expensive. Efficient indexing techniques are required that enable searches over large databases in real time without compromising accuracy. Three different indexing techniques are designed, developed, tested, and described in this book.

The fundamentals of biometric recognition, importance of indexing techniques in large-scale biometric systems and their challenges, current developments and benchmarking are discussed in Chap. 1. An efficient triangulation based indexing technique for minutiae based biometrics especially for fingerprints is described in Chap. 2. This technique use an efficient representation named extended Delaunay triangulation for the fingerprints to make the system robust against distortions. Further, the extended triangulation is classified based on the type of minutiae at the vertices of each triangle. Such classification provides better partitioning of the database, leading to a significant decrease in the number of potential matches during identification. Chapter 3 discusses an indexing technique using match scores. For each image in the database, its match scores (i.e., index code) against a set of pre-selected sample images are calculated. Then a new storage mechanism is designed for the biometric databases. Like traditional database records, the biometric images are arranged in sorted order based on their scores. A set of images which are very similar to query are retrieved during identification using a voting scheme. This results in a rapid search that takes constant time, i.e., independent of the database sizes.

A novel clustering based indexing technique using decision-level fusion is described in Chap. 4. An adaptive clustering algorithm is used that computes set of clusters in the database where each cluster is represented with an image called a 'leader'. The set of leaders is used to compute the index code. During identification, a list of similar candidates is retrieved from the clusters as well as index table. This approach retrieves multiple evidences for identification with minimal resources. Conclusions and future scope of this work are discussed in Chap. 5. This book explores new and efficient storing structures for the biometric databases. The designed indexing approaches identify a query in less time with high level of confidence. Further, the proposed storage mechanisms prove to be effective for fast and accurate retrieval. It is suggested that future work can be done in the following areas:

- All of the existing indexing approaches are experimented over the databases which are relatively small because of the unavailability of the large biometric databases for the researchers. Hence, creating and experimenting with these techniques on such large databases may be a challenging problem.
- Securing the biometric data from theft is also another important research topic in the area of biometrics due to the limited availability of the biometric traits. Further, computing the cancelable index codes for biometric identification is also a challenging problem.

Acknowledgements

"I've been blessed to find people who are smarter than I am, and they help me to execute the vision I have."—Russell Simmons

First and above all, I praise God, the almighty for providing me this opportunity and granting me the capability to proceed successfully.

Foremost, I would like to thank my advisors, Dr. MVNK Prasad and Prof. Chakravarthy Bhagvati, for their invaluable guidance and encouragement throughout my research work. My sincere thanks to Prof. Arun K. Pujari, Dean, and all the faculty members of SCIS, UoH for their encouragement and helpful suggestions. I would like to acknowledge the financial support of IDRBT (Established by RBI), Hyderabad for my doctoral study.

I would like to express my sincere gratitude to all my teachers. Without their support and encouragement, it would not have been possible for me to continue the studies and do this research. Their hard work and positive attitude is my main source of inspiration. I wish to convey my special thanks to my friends, co-researchers for their constant support and help during this journey.

Nothing would have been possible without the moral support of my parents, brothers, and sisters who have been the pillars of strength in all my endeavors. I am always deeply indebted to them for all that they had given me. I am thankful to my wife Devi, without whom it would have been impossible for me to finish this work. I really have no words to express my gratitude for all her support, encouragement, understanding, and sacrifice. Finally, I am grateful to my children Rithvik and Nithya for allowing me to snatch their time and spending it in endless hours of research work.

Acknowledgments

Contents

Abbreviations

AMI	Acuity Market Intelligence
ATM	Automatic Teller Machine
B-tree	Binary tree
CCD	Charge Coupled Device
CMC	Cumulative Match Characteristics
DCT	Discrete Cosine Transform
dpi	Dots Per Inch
FBI	Federal Bureau of Investigation
FVC	Fingerprint Verification Competition
$FVList$	List of Feature Vectors
HR	Hit Rate
IAFIS	Integrated Automated Fingerprint Identification System
$I_{id}List$	List of Image Identities
kd-tree	k Dimensional tree
kdb-tree	k-dimensional B-tree
K-L	Karhunen–Loève
k-NN	K Nearest Neighbor
LBP	Local Binary Pattern
LSH	Locality Sensitive Hashing
MBC	Minutiae Binary Code
MCC	Minutiae Cylindric Code
MR	Miss Rate
PCA	Principal Component Analysis
PolyU	Hong Kong Polytechnic University
PR	Penetration Rate
SIFT	Scale-Invariant Feature Transform
SURF	Speed-Up Robust Features
UIDAI	Unique Identification Authority of India
USD	United States Dollar
VA+	Vector Approximation +

List of Figures

List of Tables

Chapter 1
Introduction

Abstract In biometric identification systems, the identity corresponding to an individual is determined by comparing his/her template against all user templates in the database. This exhaustive matching process increases the response time and the number of false matches of the system. An effective mechanism is required that reduces the number of templates to be compared with the query during identification. Biometric indexing is such technique that limits the search space and identifies an individual in real time with high accuracy. Many authors have presented a number of biometric indexing techniques. This chapter explores the fundamentals of biometric indexing, its challenges, classifying and benchmarking along with a number of techniques proposed by various researchers.

Keywords Biometrics · Verification · Identification · Indexing · Classification

1.1 Introduction

In today's security conscious society, automatic personal authentication is important in different applications including government, commercial, educational institutions, industries, public places, etc. Questions such as "Is this the person who he claims to be?", "Should this individual be authorized to perform this transaction?", "Does this employee have authorization to access this service?" etc., are asked millions of time every day by thousands of organizations in both private and public sectors [1].

Existing systems use either identity cards or passwords for personal authentication (Fig. 1.1a). These security systems no longer suffice for individual authentication because cards can be stolen or forged and a password can be forgotten or cracked. The following are some interesting statistics:

1. According to a report by Nilson, "$11.27 billion losses due to credit card and debit card fraud during 2012" [2].
2. According to American Bankers Association's Deposit Account Fraud Survey-2011, "Financial institutions incurred $955 million in losses due to debit card fraud in 2010, which is around a 21% increase from the $788 million in losses incurred during 2008" [2].

© The Author(s) 2017   1
I. Kavati et al., *Efficient Biometric Indexing and Retrieval Techniques
for Large-Scale Systems*, SpringerBriefs in Computer Science,
DOI 10.1007/978-3-319-57660-2_1

(a)

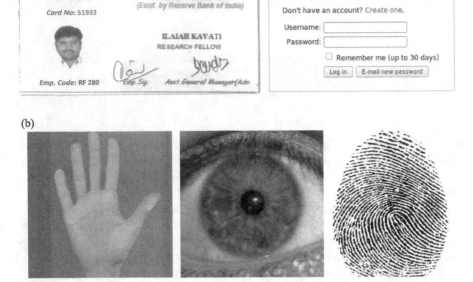

(b)

Fig. 1.1 Personal authentication techniques: **a** Traditional methods such as identity cards, Passwords, etc., **b** Biometric characteristics [16]

3. According to the Gartner Group, "between 20 to 50% of all help desk calls are for password resets and the average help desk labor cost for a single password reset is about $70" [3].

The above statistics shows the need of an accurate and efficient approach for personal recognition. Biometric recognition that uses humans fingerprint and/or palmprint and/or iris, etc., is a better choice and a reliable solution for convenient human recognition (Fig. 1.1b). As humans biometric features are unique, cannot be stolen/forgotten, and the person must be physically present during authentication [4], biometric recognition systems are gaining popularity and deployed in many important applications [5–13]. This results large-scale biometric databases in real time and an identification system need to search millions of records to identify a query. As the biometric data do not have any natural sorting order like numeric or alphabetic [14, 15], recognition in these large biometric systems is a challenging problem. In this book, we explore methods that are capable of searching biometric databases in real time with a high level of confidence.

1.2 Biometric Recognition

"A biometric system is a pattern recognition system that recognizes individuals based on the measurement of their physiological and/or behavioral traits: Physiological traits include a person's fingerprint, facial features, palmprint, vein pattern, or ocular characteristics; Behavioral traits include voice, gait, keystrokes, signature etc." [17]. The word biometrics is derived from the Greek words bios (meaning life) and metron (meaning measurement), i.e., biometric traits are the measurements from living human body. Figure 1.2 shows a few of the biometric traits (including physiological and behavioral) for personal recognition.

A generic biometric system is shown in Fig. 1.3. It consists of two modules: enrollment and recognition.

Enrollment

This module enrolls the individuals into the biometric system (Fig. 1.3a). During enrollment, a sensor captures the biometric characteristic of an individual, from which a set of features (template) are extracted by a feature extractor. Depending on the application context, the extracted feature template may be stored in a central database along with the individual's identity (name, ID number, etc.) or be recorded on a smart card issued to the individual.

Recognition

This module recognizes the identity of an individual at the point of service. During this phase, the sensor acquires the biometric characteristic of the individual to be recognized. The captured biometric image is preprocessed by the feature extractor to generate the template. The extracted template is compared to the prestored template(s) using a matcher to establish the identity. The process of user recognition in biometric systems is shown in Fig. 1.3b, c. A biometric recognition system is designed to work in one of the two different modes: (i) verification or (ii) identification.

1.2.1 Verification

In verification mode, the user will claim his identity by using a user name, or a personal identification number, or a smart card, etc., along with the biometric data. The system will then verify the user by matching the acquired biometric characteristic with his own biometric sample prestored in the system. The system in this mode, conducts a one-to-one matching to determine whether the identity claimed by the individual is true or not [18]. In this case, the question "Is Mr. X really who he claims to be?" is answered in either acceptance or rejection. An example of the verification scenario occurs when we try to use the ATM at a bank. We have to provide our biometric data along with ATM card to verify our identity. In this case, the system

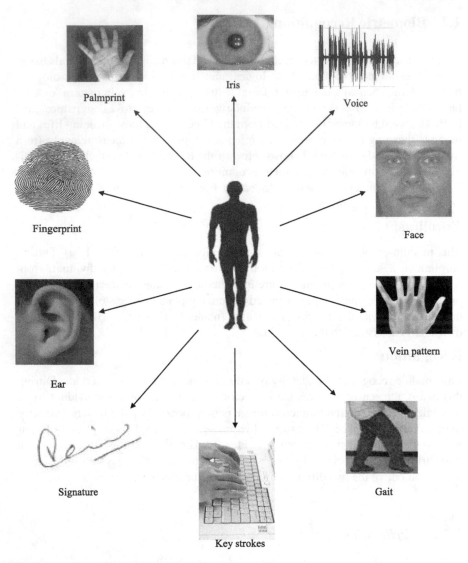

Fig. 1.2 Different biometric traits for personal recognition

compares the provided biometric data with our prestored template to ensure that the true owner is the one who is using the card to perform the transaction. The process of recognizing a user in verification mode can be seen in Fig. 1.3b.

1.2.2 Identification

In this mode, the user does not claim any identity. The user provides his biometric data, and the data is compared to the stored template of every individual in the system database. The system in this mode, conducts a one-to-many comparison to find the identity of an individual. In this case, the question "To whom does the submitted biometric data belong?" is answered. For example, if a fingerprint impression is found at a crime scene, to determine the suspect it is compared to all the enrolled fingerprints in the database. If a match is found, the identity of the suspect is determined. The process of recognizing a user in identification mode can be seen in Fig. 1.3c.

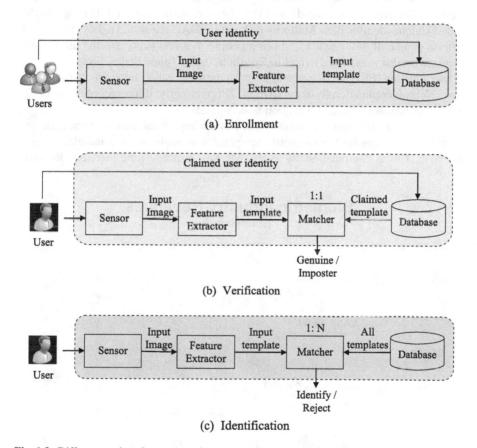

(a) Enrollment

(b) Verification

(c) Identification

Fig. 1.3 Different modes of operation of a generic biometric system [16]

1.3   Indexing

In today's security conscious society, biometric recognition systems became more popular and deployed in variety of applications such as surveillance, border control, network access, banking, employee authentication, etc. The market for biometric applications is growing worldwide, and specifically in emerging economies, such as India, where scalability is a huge challenge. According to a market research report by Acuity Market Intelligence (AMI) [19], the market for worldwide biometrics industry is expected to grow steadily from an annual revenue of 3.4 billion USD in 2009 to 11 billion USD in 2017 as shown in Fig. 1.4.

Note that, most of these biometric systems deal with large-scale databases and their size is increasing at a rapid pace. For instance, India's national ID program [5] called Unique Identification Authority of India (UIDAI) registered a database of 700 million people. It will reach 1.25 billion people in a few years and the number of accesses per day is expected to be 1 to 5 million. In the United States, Federal Bureau of Investigation (FBI) developed a fingerprint database called Integrated Automated Fingerprint Identification System (IAFIS) [20]. Currently, it has records of over 51 million criminals and over 1.5 million noncriminals.

However, identification of an individual in such large databases is typically determined by matching his/her biometric template with each enrolled template in the database. This is computationally expensive, i.e., response time increases linearly

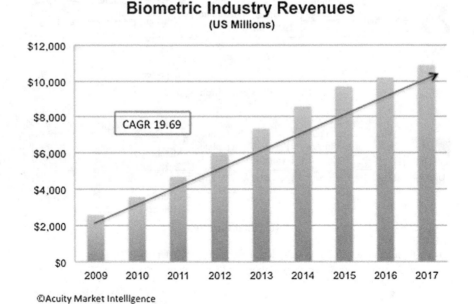

Fig. 1.4   Acuity Market Intelligence (AMI) Report

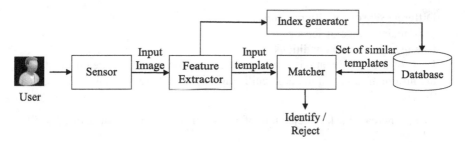

Fig. 1.5 Process of Biometric identification using indexing approach [16]

with size of the database. Hence, there is a need of efficient retrieval methods that can enable searches in reduced space of the database and thus reduces the search time without compromising accuracy.

This **problem**, i.e., **search space reduction in biometric databases** may be stated as follows: *Given a large biometric database D and a query q, the identification system has to,*

- Quickly retrieve a candidate set C from D such that the retrieved images in C are most similar to q,
- $|C| \ll |D|$, and
- C must contain q's identity with high probability.

There are two different approaches to handle this problem. The first one is partitioning the images stored in the database [21]. The entire database is divided into small number of partitions, i.e., classes. To identify a query, first its class is determined and compared only with the candidates of that class to which the query belongs. However, this approach uses only predefined classes and the images are unevenly distributed among them resulting in variation in the system performance [4]. Further, the system must handle rejected templates carefully.

The second approach is indexing which computes an index to every individual (Fig. 1.5). To identify a query, this technique retrieves a set of similar candidates from the database whose index are most similar to it. Next the query is compared only with the retrieved similar candidates instead of with the complete database and thus reduces the search space.

1.3.1 Challenges

The following are few issues that need to be considered while indexing.

- Intra-class variations, i.e., two images of the same user obtained at different time instances may not be same. This is mainly because of,

- Different sensors at different times.
- Poor maintenance of sensors.
- Changes in lighting conditions.
- Lack of user cooperation. For example, a person may have beard or glasses at enrollment time but not at identification time; different facial expressions at different times.

This may increase the false rejections of the system as different indexes are possible for the same user.
- Inter-class similarity, i.e., overlap of feature space of different users leads to increase in false matches.
- Further, indexing methods of relational databases are also not suitable for biometric data [14, 15]. In relational databases, records (or data) are arranged in an alphabetical or numerical order with respect to a primary key for efficient retrieval. But biometric templates do not have any sorting order to arrange [14, 15].
- Finally, the indexing methods for multimedia (i.e., image, video) databases are also not suitable for biometric databases [22–31]. The following are a few reasons:

    - In multimedia databases, there is large variability among the subjects in terms of appearance i.e., different type of subjects (like trees, humans, buildings, etc.) are present in the database. Hence, a coarse-level classification is possible. But, there is little appearance variability among the biometric images of different users, i.e., the biometric samples of different users look almost similar. For example, in a fingerprint database, the impressions of different users almost look similar with few differences.
    - The multimedia (especially image and video) data are represented with metadata [31] such as annotated text, symbols, tags, etc., which is not possible for biometric data.
    - Finally, the feature representation of biometric data is different from multimedia data [32]. Basically, the multimedia data is represented with texture [24, 27–29], color [22, 23, 25] and shape [26] features. However, most of the biometric characteristics do not contain these features.

1.4   Biometric Indexing Techniques

The fast identification in biometric databases can be achieved by two different approaches: classification and indexing. These approaches are used to filter the search space during identification process. In classification approaches, the database images are divided into different groups (classes) such that the images in the same class are similar in terms of some quantitative information. During identification, the class of the query is first identified and then it is matched with only the images present in that class. However, as said earlier, these approaches have a serious limitation that the images are unevenly distributed among the predefined classes which makes the system statistically unreliable for faster identification.

In indexing approaches, each image is assigned an index based on its features. During identification, the query is matched with only the images which have similar index. Majority of current developments for biometric indexing are based on one of the following features:

1. Key feature points [33–42]
2. Geometric properties of Triplets [18, 43–48]
3. Match scores [49–54]
4. Other approaches

   - Ridge orientation based (for fingerprint) [55–58]
   - Texture based (for palmprint [59–62], iris [32, 63, 64])
   - Color based (for iris) [65–67]
   - Subspace approximations (for face) [68–70].

1.4.1   Key Feature Point Based Indexing Approaches

These approaches extract the key feature points from the biometric samples and use them for indexing purpose. Boro et al. [33] developed an indexing technique using fingerprint minutiae points (i.e., bifurcation and end points). The minutiae features are enrolled into a hash table using geometric hashing [71]. Jayaraman et al. [36] proposed a minutiae-based geometric hashing technique for fingerprint indexing. A fixed length feature vector called Minutiae Binary Code (MBC) is computed for each minutia in the fingerprint. The minutiae and its feature vector are stored into the hash table using geometric hashing.

Mansukhani et al. proposed an indexing approach based on minutiae tree [34]. They constructed a large index tree where the enrolled templates are represented by the leaves of the tree. The branches in the index tree correspond to different local configurations of minutiae points. Searching the index tree entails extracting local minutiae neighborhoods of the test fingerprint and matching them against tree nodes. Cappelli et al. developed Minutiae Cylinder-Code (MCC) based indexing technique [35]. For each fingerprint, a fixed size binary code is computed. This code is a representation of spatial and directional relationships between a minutia and its neighborhood structure with a minutiae cylinder. To find the best matches, Locality Sensitive Hashing (LSH) technique is used.

Badrinath et al. [37] propose an efficient indexing scheme using geometric hashing of Speeded Up Robust Features (SURF) [72] to index the palmprint into a hash table. During querying, a score-level fusion of voting strategy based on geometric hashing and SURF score is used to identify the live palmprint. In a recent work, Dewangan et al. [39] proposes a face indexing method based on SURF key features and k-d tree. Authors created a two-level index space based on the SURF key points and divide the index space into a number of cells. Further, they define a set of hash functions to store the SURF descriptors of a face image into the cell. The SURF descriptors within an index cell are stored into k-d tree.

Table 1.1 Key feature point based indexing approaches

Author	Features used	Approach	Biometric
Boro and Roy (2004), [33]	Minutiae features	Geometric hashing	Fingerprint
Jayaraman et al. (2014) [36]	Minutiae features	Geometric hashing and Minutiae binary code	Fingerprint
Mansukhani et al.(2010), [34]	Minutiae features	Minutiae tree	Fingerprint
Cappelli et al. (2010), [35]	Minutiae features	Minutiae cylinder-code and Locality sensitive hashing	Fingerprint
Badrinath et al. (2013), [37]	SURF features	Geometric hashing and fusion	Palmprint
Dewangan et al. (2013), [39]	SURF features	kd- tree	Face
Mehrotra et al. (2010), [40]	SIFT features	Geometric hashing	Iris
Panda et al. (2013), [41]	SIFT features	Parallel geometric hashing	Iris
Mehrotra et al. (2013), [42]	SIFT features	k–d–b tree	Iris

Mehrotra et al. [40] proposed an indexing method based on Scale Invariant Feature Transform (SIFT) [73]. The SIFT features are extracted for each iris image and mapped into a hash table using geometric hashing. Panda et al. [41] proposed an indexing method for iris databases using parallel geometric hashing. Authors first, extract the SIFT features from the iris images. The SIFT features are indexed into a hash table using a parallel geometric hashing using multiple processors. The use of parallel processors increases the retrieval performance of the system during identification. In another work, Mehrotra et al. [42] also used the SIFT features for iris indexing. The extracted SIFT features are indexed using a k-d-b tree. During identification, a range search is used to retrieve a set of similar images to the query. The summary of different key feature point based indexing techniques is given Table 1.1.

1.4.2   Triplet-Based Indexing Approaches

These approaches compute some form of triplets using the feature points of the biometric samples for indexing purpose. Bhanu and Tan [43] proposed a triplet-based fingerprint indexing method. They compute all the possible triplets from the extracted minutiae of a fingerprint. Their method used triangle features such as handedness, type, direction, etc. to compute the index. Instead of all possible triangulation, Bebis et al. used Delaunay triangulation [74] of minutiae points for indexing fingerprints [44]. For each triplet of the fingerprint, their method computes the ratios of largest side of the triplet with the two smallest sides and the angle between the smallest sides to generate the index.

Ross and Mukherjee [45] also developed an indexing technique based on Delaunay triangles. However, they added ridge curvature to the minutiae triplets for improved performance. Further, they used k-means clustering for indexing the triplets. Another Delaunay triangulation-based indexing approach was proposed by Liang et al. [18]. However, this approach uses lower order Delaunay triangulation [75]. They proved that the Delaunay triangulation is sensitive to skin distortion and the order-0, order-1 Delaunay triangles are more stable and robust against distortion. Further, Alonso et al. [46] extended the Delaunay triangulation to handle the distortions caused by spurious and missing minutiae. Iloanusi et al. [48] proposed a minutiae quadruplet based approach for fingerprint indexing. The authors used multiple fingers of an individual and extracted the geometric information from the minutiae quadruplets. Four, five, and ten fingerprints from a subject are fused at the rank level using the highest rank rule.

Jayaraman et al. [47] also proposed a method for palmprint indexing using SURF features. They extract the SURF features from each palm image. Then they apply a series of preprocessing steps on the SURF features, such as, mean centering, principal component analysis, rotation, and normalization to make them invariant to affine transformations. Finally, a block-based triangulation is applied and the geometric features of the triangles are indexed using geometric hashing. Table 1.2 shows the summary of various triplet-based indexing approaches.

1.4.3 Match Score Based Indexing Approaches

These approaches use the match score between the images for indexing purpose. The first such attempt was made by Maeda et al. [49]. A match score vector was calculated for each image by matching it against all the images in the database and stored. During identification, the match score vector of the query is compared against each image score vector.

Table 1.2 Triplet-based indexing approaches

Author	Features used	Approach	Biometric
Bhanu and Tan (2003), [43]	Minutiae triplets	All possible triangle	Fingerprint
Bebis et al. (1999), [44]	Minutiae triplets	Delaunay triangulation	Fingerprint
Ross and Mukherjee (2007), [45]	Minutiae triplets and ridge curvature	k- means clustering	Fingerprint
Liang et al. (2007), [18]	Minutiae neighborhood and minutiae triplets	Delaunay triangulation	Fingerprint
Alonso et al. (2013), [46]	Minutiae triplets	Extended triangulation	Fingerprint
Iloanusi et al. (2014), [48]	Minutiae quadruplets	Clustering	Fingerprint
Jayaraman et al. (2013), [47]	Triangulation of normalized SURF features	Modified geometric hashing	Palmprint

Table 1.3 Match score based indexing approaches

Author	Features used	Approach	Biometric
Maeda et al. (2004), [49]	Match score	Linear search	Fingerprint
Gyaourova and Ross (2012), [51]	Match scores	Linear search and correlation	Multimodal (Face, Fingerprint)
Paliwal et al. (2010), [52]	Match scores	VA+ file	Palmprint
Kavati et al. (2014a), [53]	Match scores	Voting	Palmprint
Kavati et al. (2014b), [54]	Match scores	Voting and leader clustering	Palmprint

Gyaourova and Ross [51] present an indexing approach based on match scores. This method generates a set of match scores called index code, by comparing a biometric image with a small set of reference images. During querying, the match scores between the test image and all the enrolled images are compared to identify the candidate list. This approach was tested individually on face and fingerprint database. Finally, the candidate identities from both the databases are fused to identify the best matches. Authors claim that comparison of two score vectors takes less time compared to matching two templates.

Paliwal et al. [52] proposed another work based on match scores. For each image, a set of match scores are computed like Gyaourova and Ross [51] method. The computed match scores are stored into a Vector Approximation (VA+) file which is a space partitioning method. This method use k-NN search and texture to retrieve top k similar matches. This approach was tested on a palmprint database. Table 1.3 shows the summary of the various score based indexing approaches.

1.4.4   Other Indexing Approaches

In the literature, there are also some indexing techniques for biometric systems which are based on different features other than discussed above. For example, ridge information for fingerprints; texture, color information for palmprints, iris and face biometrics, etc. Summary of other indexing techniques in the literature are given in Table 1.4.

1.5   Benchmarking in Indexing and Performance Evaluation

Benchmarking is the process of validating the results and comparing with already existing best practices in the literature. The benchmarking improves the quality of the development activity. Some of the biometric benchmark databases (like PolyU palm-

Table 1.4 Other indexing approaches

Author	Features used	Approach	Biometric
Lumini et al. (1997), [55]	Reduced dimensional directional image	K-L transform and continuous classification	Fingerprint
Lee et al. (2005), [56]	Ridge orientation, interridge spacing	Feature map and PCA	Fingerprint
Jiang et al. (2006), [57]	Ridge orientation, dominant ridge distance	Hierarchical based	Fingerprint
Cappelli (2011), [58]	Ridge orientation and ridge line frequencies	Weighted fusion of scores	Fingerprint
You et al. (2002), [59]	Global texture energy and interesting points	Multifeature hierarchical	Palmprint
You et al. (2004), [60]	Global texture energy, fuzzy interest line and local directional texture energy features	Multifeature coding based	Palmprint
Li et al. (2005), [61]	Global texture energy and local texture energy	Multifeature hierarchical	Palmprint
Mukherjee and Ross (2008), [63]	Gabor wavelet IrisCode features	PCA and k-means clustering	Iris
Mehrotra et al. (2009), [64]	DCT energy histogram features	B-tree	Iris
Dey et al. (2012), [32]	Gabor energy features	Hashing	Iris
Fu et al. (2005), [65]	Maximum response from an artificial color filter	Color based classification	Iris
Puhan and Sudha (2008), [66]	Blue and red color indices	Color based classification	Iris
Jayaraman et al. (2012), [67]	Color and SURF features	kd-tree	Iris
Kyperountas et al. (2008), [68]	Discriminant projected face data	Clustering	Face
Lin et al. (2003), [69]	Eigenfaces and PCA	Condensed database	Face
Mohanty et al. (2008), [70]	Linear subspace based match scores	k-NN search	Face

print, FVC fingerprint) are available to the research community for evaluation. The performance of the indexing algorithm can be calculated based on various parameters like hit rate and penetration rate.

1.5.1 Databases

Experiments are conducted on the following biometric databases:

1. Fingerprint Verification Competition (FVC) databases
2. PolyU Palmprint database

These databases exhibit some fundamental differences such as type of biometric, device used to capture the images, resolution, lighting conditions, etc. This forms the basis for the study of the proposed work under different circumstances. Detailed description of these databases is given in the following:

1.5.1.1   Fingerprint Verification Competition (FVC) Databases

The seven FVC databases used in the experiments are: 1. FVC 2002 DB1, 2. FVC 2002 DB2, 3. FVC 2002 DB3, 4. FVC 2002 DB4, 5. FVC 2004 DB1, 6. FVC 2004 DB2, and 7. FVC 2004 DB4. Each of these database comprises images from 100 different fingers. Each finger has 8 impressions in the database. This makes a total of 800 images to perform the experiments. Further, each database is divided into two mutually exclusive training (i.e., *Gallery*) and test (i.e., *Probe*) sets. Arbitrarily, four images per finger are chosen for training and the remaining four images are used for testing.

1.5.1.2   PolyU Palmprint Database

The PolyU palmprint database was acquired at the Hong Kong Polytechnic University using a CCD (Charge Coupled Device) camera [76] at a spatial resolution of 75 dpi and 256 gray levels. This benchmark database consists of 7,752 grayscale images of size 384×284 pixels corresponding to 386 different palms. Around 20 images per palm have been collected in two sessions. Arbitrarily 10 images per palm are considered for training and remaining 10 images are used for testing. Table 1.5 shows the detailed description of each database used in the experiments.

1.5.2 Performance Metrics

The performance of the proposed indexing approaches is determined using the following measures:

Table 1.5 Characteristics of the databases used in the experiments

Database	Size	Sensor	Image size	Subjects	Samples	Resolution (dpi)
FVC 2002 DB1	800	Optical sensor	388×374	100	8	500
FVC 2002 DB2	800	Optical sensor	296×560	100	8	569
FVC 2002 DB3	800	Capacitive sensor	300×300	100	8	500
FVC 2002 DB4	800	Synthetic	288×384	100	8	≈ 500
FVC 2004 DB1	800	Optical sensor	640×480	100	8	500
FVC 2004 DB2	800	Optical sensor	328×364	100	8	500
FVC 2004 DB4	800	Synthetic	288×384	100	8	≈ 500
PolyU palmprint	7752	CCD camera	384×284	386	≈ 20	75

1. Hit Rate (HR)
2. Miss Rate (MR)
3. Penetration Rate (PR)
4. Cumulative Match Characteristics (CMC) curve

1.5.2.1 Hit Rate (HR):

Hit Rate (HR) is the percentage of test set images for which the corresponding gallery set image with the correct match is present in the retrieved candidate set.

$$HR = \left(\frac{y}{M}\right) \times 100\% \tag{1.1}$$

where y is the correctly identified test set images and M is the total number of test set images.

1.5.2.2 Miss Rate (MR):

Miss Rate (MR) is the percentage of probe set images for which the corresponding gallery set image with the correct match is not present in the candidate set.

$$MR = 100 - HR \tag{1.2}$$

1.5.2.3 Penetration Rate (PR):

Penetration Rate (PR) is the average percentage of gallery set images retrieved (i.e., Candidate set) to identify a query image from the test set by the indexing mechanism.

$$PR = \left(\frac{1}{M} \sum_{i=1}^{M} \frac{|C^i|}{N} \right) \times 100\% \tag{1.3}$$

where C^i is the candidate set of the ith test set image, N is the number of images in the gallery set, and M is number of images in the test set.

An efficient indexing method will have a high hit rate (low miss rate) and a low penetration rate.

1.5.2.4 Cumulative Match Characteristics (CMC) Curve

CMC curves represent the identification accuracy of the system at various ranks. To determine the accuracy, the images in the retrieved candidate set are sorted in descending order such that the image in the first position is most similar to the query and other positions are arranged accordingly. We assign rank 1 to the image in candidate set at the first position, rank 2 to the image at the second position, and so on. Accuracy at rank n (denoted by I_n) indicates the percentage of test set images for which the genuine match is present in top n images of the sorted candidate set. This is formulated in Eq. 1.4, where z denote the number of test set images for which the genuine match is in top n, and M denote the total number of images in the test set.

$$I_n = \frac{z}{M} \tag{1.4}$$

1.6 Summary

The chapter includes a brief introduction to biometric recognition and importance of indexing. It also explored different issues that should be addressed by an indexing system. The current developments in the field of biometric indexing and retrieval also explored. Finally the benchmarking, and performance evaluation procedures for biometric indexing techniques are explained.

References

1. A.K. JAIN, P. FLYNN, AND A. ROSS. *Handbook of biometrics*. Springer, 2007.
2. **Credit Card and Debit Card Fraud Statistic**. http://www.cardhub.com/edu/credit-debit-card-fraud-statistics, May 2014.
3. **Password Cost Estimater**. http://www.mandylionlabs.com/PRCCalc/PRCCalc.htm, May 2014.
4. D. MALTONI, D. MAIO, A.K. JAIN, AND S. PRABHAKAR. *Handbook of Fingerprint Recognition*. Springer, 2nd edition, 2009.
5. AADHAAR. **Unique Identification Authority of India**. http://uidai.gov.in/, July 2014.

6. **Singapore Immigration and Checkpoint authority**. http://www.ica.gov.sg/page.aspx?pageid=407, september 2014.
7. CROSSING U.S. BORDERS. http://www.dhs.gov/crossing-us-borders, July 2014.
8. FIND BIOMETRICS. **Mobile Biometrics, PDAs & Laptop Fingerprint Readers**. http://findbiometrics.com/applications/mobile-biometrics/, september 2014.
9. PLANET BIOMETRICS. **Physical Access and Attendence**. http://www.planetbiometrics.com/physical-access/, september 2014.
10. **Iris Scans at Amsterdam Airport Schiphol**. http://www.schiphol.nl/Travellers/AtSchiphol/Privium/Privium/IrisScans.htm, september 2014.
11. **United Arab Emirates Deployment of Iris Recognition:**. http://www.cl.cam.ac.uk/~jgd1000/deployments.html, July 2014.
12. TSA. **Transportation Security Administration**. http://www.tsa.gov/, september 2014.
13. J. HAMMOND. **Biometric traveler screening introduced in Orlando, Denver next**. http://www.examiner.com/article/biometric-traveler-screening-introduced-orlando-denver-next/, september 2014.
14. A. MHATRE, S. PALLA, S. CHIKKERUR, AND V. GOVINDARAJU. **Efficient search and retrieval in biometric databases**. In *Society of Photo-Optical Instrumentation Engineers proceedings series*, pages 265–273, 2005.
15. A. MHATRE, S. CHIKKERUR, AND V. GOVINDARAJU. **Indexing biometric databases using pyramid technique**. In *Audio-and Video-Based Biometric Person Authentication*, pages 841–849, 2005.
16. ILAIAH KAVATI, MUNAGA VNK PRASAD, AND CHAKRAVARTHY BHAGVATI. **Search Space Reduction in Biometric Databases: A Review**. *Developing Next-Generation Countermeasures for Homeland Security Threat Prevention*, page 236, 2016.
17. A.K. JAIN, A. ROSS, AND K. NANDAKUMAR. *Introduction to biometrics*. Springer, 2011.
18. X. LIANG, A BISHNU, AND T. ASANO. **A Robust Fingerprint Indexing Scheme Using Minutia Neighborhood Structure and Low-Order Delaunay Triangles**. *IEEE Transactions on Information Forensics and Security*, 2(4):721–733, 2007.
19. ACUITY. **The Future of Biometrics Market Research Report**. http://www.acuitymi.com/FOBReport.php, september 2014.
20. FBI. **Integrated Automated Fingerprint Identification System**. http://www.fbi.gov/about-us/cjis/fingerprintsbiometrics/iafis/iafis, september 2014.
21. E. HENRY. *Classification and Uses of Finger Prints*. Routledge, London, 1900.
22. G.H. LIU AND J.Y. YANG. **Content-based image retrieval using color difference histogram**. *Pattern Recognition*, 46(1):188–198, 2013.
23. Y. D. CHUN, N. C. KIM, AND I. H. JANG. **Content-Based Image Retrieval Using Multiresolution Color and Texture Features**. *IEEE Transactions on Multimedia*, 10(6):1073–1084, 2008.
24. H.A. MOGHADDAM AND M.N. DEHAJI. **Enhanced Gabor wavelet correlogram feature for image indexing and retrieval**. *Pattern Analysis and Applications*, 16(2):163–177, 2013.
25. J. HUANG, S.R. KUMAR, M. MITRA, W.J. ZHU, AND R. ZABIH. **Image Indexing Using Color Correlograms**. In *Proceedings of the Conference on Computer Vision and Pattern Recognition (CVPR)*, pages 762–768, 1997.
26. S. BERRETTI, A.D. BIMBO, AND P. PALA. **Retrieval by Shape Similarity with Perceptual Distance and Effective Indexing**. *IEEE Transactions on Multimedia*, 2(4):225–239, 2000.
27. M.K. MANDAL, T. ABOULNASR, AND S. PANCHANATHAN. **Fast wavelet histogram techniques for image indexing**. In *Proceedings of IEEE Workshop on Content-Based Access of Image and Video Libraries*, pages 68–72, Jun 1998.
28. H.A MOGHADDAM AND M.S. TARZJAN. **Gabor Wavelet Correlogram Algorithm for Image Indexing and Retrieval**. In *18th International Conference on Pattern Recognition*, 2, pages 925–928, 2006.
29. B. S. MANJUNATH AND W. Y. MA. **Texture Features for Browsing and Retrieval of Image Data**. *IEEE Trans. Pattern Anal. Mach. Intell.*, 18(8):837–842, 1996.

30. J. VLEUGELS AND R.C. VELTKAMP. **Efficient image retrieval through vantage objects.** *Pattern Recognition*, 35(1):69–80, 2002.

31. J. JEON, V. LAVRENKO, AND R. MANMATHA. **Automatic Image Annotation and Retrieval Using Cross-media Relevance Models.** In *International ACM SIGIR Conference on Research and Development in Informaion Retrieval*, pages 119–126, 2003.

32. S. DEY AND D. SAMANTA. **Iris data indexing method using gabor energy features.** *IEEE Transactions on Information Forensics and Security*, 7(4):1192–1203, 2012.

33. R. BORO AND S.D. ROY. **Fast and Robust Projective Matching for Fingerprints Using Geometric Hashing.** In *Indian Conference on Computer Vision, Graphics and Image Processing*, pages 681–688, 2004.

34. P. MANSUKHANI, S. TULYAKOV, AND V. GOVINDARAJU. **A Framework for Efficient Fingerprint Identification Using a Minutiae Tree.** *IEEE Systems Journal*, 4(2):126–137, 2010.

35. R. CAPPELLI, M. FERRARA, AND D. MALTONI. **Minutia Cylinder-Code: A New Representation and Matching Technique for Fingerprint Recognition.** *IEEE Transactions on Pattern Analysis and Machine Intelligence*, 32(12):2128–2141, 2010.

36. U. JAYARAMAN, A.K. GUPTA, AND P. GUPTA. **An efficient minutiae based geometric hashing for fingerprint database.** *Neurocomputing*, 137:115–126, 2014.

37. G.S. BADRINATH, P. GUPTA, AND H. MEHROTRA. **Score level fusion of voting strategy of geometric hashing and SURF for an efficient palmprint-based identification.** *Journal of real-time image processing*, 8(3):265–284, 2013.

38. V.D. KAUSHIK, U. JAYARAMAN, A.K. GUPTA, A.K. GUPTA, AND P. GUPTA. **An efficient indexing scheme for face database using modified geometric hashing.** *Neurocomputing*, 116:208–221, 2013.

39. J. DEWANGAN, S. DEY, AND D. SAMANTA. **Face Images Database Indexing for Person Identification Problem.** *International Journal of Biometrics and Bioinformatics*, 7(2):93–122, 2013.

40. H. MEHROTRA, B. MAJHI, AND P. GUPTA. **Robust iris indexing scheme using geometric hashing of SIFT keypoints.** *Journal of Network and Computer Applications*, 33(3):300–313, 2010.

41. A.C. PANDA, H. MEHROTRA, AND B. MAJHI. **Parallel geometric hashing for robust iris indexing.** *Journal of real-time image processing*, 8(3):341–349, 2013.

42. H. MEHROTRA AND B. MAJHI. **An efficient indexing scheme for iris biometric using kdb trees.** In *Intelligent Computing Theories and Technology*, pages 475–484. 2013.

43. B. BHANU AND X. TAN. **Fingerprint indexing based on novel features of minutiae triplets.** *IEEE Transactions on Pattern Analysis and Machine Intelligence*, 25(5):616–622, 2003.

44. G. BEBIS, T. DEACONU, AND M. GEORGIOPOULOS. **Fingerprint Identification Using Delaunay Triangulation.** In *International Conference on Information, Intelligence, and Systems*, pages 452–452, 1999.

45. A. ROSS AND R. MUKHERJEE. **Augmenting ridge curves with minutiae triplets for fingerprint indexing.** In *Defense and Security Symposium*, pages 65390C–65390C. International Society for Optics and Photonics, 2007.

46. A.G. ALONSO, J.H. PALANCAR, E.R. REINA, AND A.M. BRISEO. **Indexing and retrieving in fingerprint databases under structural distortions.** *Expert Systems with Applications*, 40(8):2858–2871, 2013.

47. U. JAYARAMAN, S. PRAKASH, AND P. GUPTA. **Use of geometric features of principal components for indexing a biometric database.** *Mathematical and Computer Modelling*, 58(1):147–164, 2013.

48. O.N. ILOANUSI. **Fusion of finger types for fingerprint indexing using minutiae quadruplets.** *Pattern Recognition Letters*, 38:8–14, 2014.

49. T. MAEDA, M. MATSUSHITA, AND K. SASAKAWA. **Characteristics of the Identification Algorithm Using a Matching Score Matrix.** In *ICBA*, pages 330–336, 2004.

50. A. GYAOUROVA AND A. ROSS. **A novel coding scheme for indexing fingerprint patterns.** In *Structural, Syntactic, and Statistical Pattern Recognition*, pages 755–764. 2008.

51. A. GYAOUROVA AND A. ROSS. **Index Codes for Multibiometric Pattern Retrieval.** *IEEE Transactions on Information Forensics and Security*, 7(2):518–529, 2012.

52. A. PALIWAL, U. JAYARAMAN, AND P. GUPTA. **A score based indexing scheme for palm-print databases.** In *International Conference on Image Processing*, pages 2377–2380, 2010.

53. MUNAGA V N K PRASAD ILAIAH KAVATI AND CHAKRAVARTHY BHAGVATI. **An Efficient Coding Method for Indexing Hand Based Biometric Databases.** In *International Conference on Artificial Intelligence and Evolutionary Algorithms in Engineering Systems*, pages 723–731, 2014.

54. MUNAGA V N K PRASAD ILAIAH KAVATI AND CHAKRAVARTHY BHAGVATI. **A New Indexing Method for Biometric Databases using Match Scores and Decision-Level Fusion.** In *International Conference on Advanced Computing, Networking and Informatics*, pages 493–500, 2014.

55. A. LUMINI, D. MAIO, AND D. MALTONI. **Continuous versus exclusive classification for fingerprint retrieval.** *Pattern Recognition Letters*, 18(10):1027–1034, 1997.

56. S.O. LEE, Y.G. KIM, AND G.T. PARK. **A Feature Map Consisting of Orientation and Inter-ridge Spacing for Fingerprint Retrieval.** In *5th International Conference on Audio- and Video-Based Biometric Person Authentication*, pages 184–190, 2005.

57. X. JIANG, M. LIU, AND A.C. KOT. **Fingerprint Retrieval for Identification.** *IEEE Transactions on Information Forensics and Security*, 1(4):532–542, 2006.

58. R. CAPPELLI. **Fast and accurate fingerprint indexing based on ridge orientation and frequency.** *IEEE Transactions on Systems, Man, and Cybernetics, Part B: Cybernetics*, 41(6):1511–1521, 2011.

59. J. YOU, W. LI, AND D. ZHANG. **Hierarchical palmprint identification via multiple feature extraction.** *Pattern recognition*, 35(4):847–859, 2002.

60. J. YOU, W.K. KONG, D. ZHANG, AND K.H. CHEUNG. **On hierarchical palmprint coding with multiple features for personal identification in large databases.** *IEEE Transactions on Circuits and Systems for Video Technology*, 14(2):234–243, 2004.

61. W. LI, J. YOU, AND D. ZHANG. **Texture-based palmprint retrieval using a layered search scheme for personal identification.** *IEEE Transactions on Multimedia*, 7(5):891–898, 2005.

62. F. YUE, W. ZUO, D. ZHANG, AND B. LI. **Fast palmprint identification with multiple templates per subject.** *Pattern recognition letters*, 32(8):1108–1118, 2011.

63. R. MUKHERJEE AND A. ROSS. **Indexing iris images.** In *International Conference on Pattern Recognition*, pages 1–4, 2008.

64. H. MEHROTRA, G.S. BADRINATH, B. MAJHI, AND P. GUPTA. **Indexing iris biometric database using energy histogram of DCT subbands.** In *Contemporary Computing*, pages 194–204, 2009.

65. J. FU, H.J. CAULFIELD, S.M. YOO, AND V. ATLURI. **Use of artificial color filtering to improve iris recognition and searching.** *Pattern Recognition Letters*, 26(14):2244–2251, 2005.

66. N.B. PUHAN AND N. SUDHA. **A novel iris database indexing method using the iris color.** In *Conference on Industrial Electronics and Applications*, pages 1886–1891, 2008.

67. U. JAYARAMAN, S. PRAKASH, AND P. GUPTA. **An efficient color and texture based iris image retrieval technique.** *Expert Systems with Applications*, 39(5):4915–4926, 2012.

68. M. KYPEROUNTAS, A. TEFAS, AND I. PITAS. **Dynamic training using multistage clustering for face recognition.** *Pattern Recognition*, 41(3):894–905, 2008.

69. K.H LIN, K.M. LAM, X. XIE, AND W.C. SIU. **An efficient human face indexing scheme using eigenfaces.** In *International Conference on Neural Networks and Signal Processing*, 2, pages 920–923, 2003.

70. P. MOHANTY, S. SARKAR, R. KASTURI, AND P.J. PHILLIPS. **Subspace Approximation of Face Recognition Algorithms: An Empirical Study.** *IEEE Transactions on Information Forensics and Security*, 3(4):734–748, 2008.

71. Y. LAMDAN AND H.J. WOLFSON. **Geometric hashing: A general and efficient model-based recognition scheme.** In *ICCV*, 88, pages 238–249, 1988.

72. H. BAY, T. TUYTELAARS, AND LUC VAN GOOL. **Surf: Speeded up robust features**. In *Computer Vision–ECCV*, pages 404–417. 2006.

73. D.G. LOWE. **Distinctive Image Features from Scale-Invariant Keypoints**. *International Journal of Computer Vision*, **60**(2):91–110, 2004.

74. M.D. BERG, M.V. KREVELD, M. OVERMARS, AND O.C. SCHWARZKOPF. *Computational geometry*. Springer, 2000.

75. M. ABELLANAS, P. BOSE, J. GARCÍA-LÓPEZ, F. HURTADO, M. NICOLÁS, AND P.A. RAMOS. **On properties of higher-order Delaunay graphs with applications**. In *Europian Workshop on Computational Geometry*, pages 119–122, 2005.

76. M. WONG, D. ZHANG, W.K. KONG, AND G. LU. **Real-time palmprint acquisition system design**. *IEE Proceedings Vision, Image and Signal Processing,*, **152**(5):527–534, 2005.

Chapter 2
Hierarchical Decomposition of Extended Triangulation for Fingerprint Indexing

Abstract In biometric identification systems, the identity corresponding to the query image is determined by comparing it against all images in the database. This exhaustive matching process increases the response time and the number of false positives of the system. This chapter presents an efficient indexing algorithm for fingerprint databases to improve the search speed and accuracy of identification. A variant of Delaunay triangulation called extended triangulation is used to make the system robust against distortions. Then the triangles are partitioned into groups such that the retrieval algorithm searches in reduced space of the database. Experiments are conducted on different fingerprint databases, and the results show that while maintaining high hit rate the proposed method achieves lower penetration rate than what existing methods achieve.

Keywords Fingerprint · Delaunay triangulation · Extended triangulation · Hierarchical decomposition

2.1 Introduction

Nowadays, the increasing use of biometrics for personal identification in various applications has lead to increase of some large-scale biometric databases in real time [1–9]. However, identifying a user on such huge databases using a linear matching process makes the system extremely slow. Boro et al. [10] extracted the minutiae points of the fingerprints and mapped them into a hash table using geometric hashing [11]. Similarly, Hunny et al. [12] extracted the key features of iris using scale invariant feature transform [13, 14] and mapped them with the help of geometric hashing. However, the above methods require high computational and memory costs as each feature is inserted multiple times into the hash table to handle the intra-class natural variations. The triplets have been successfully used to index biometric databases [15, 16]. The triplet-based techniques have proven more powerful than point-based techniques, as the uncertainty of feature points and intra-class natural variations do not affect the angles of a triangle. In this chapter, we propose an efficient triangulation-based approach for indexing fingerprint databases. This work enhances the Delaunay triangulation to make the system robust against biometric distortions.

© The Author(s) 2017

I. Kavati et al., *Efficient Biometric Indexing and Retrieval Techniques for Large-Scale Systems*, SpringerBriefs in Computer Science, DOI 10.1007/978-3-319-57660-2_2

2.2 Indexing Framework

The proposed indexing approach follows these steps: extraction of minutiae features from fingerprint images. Then, for each fingerprint, its Delaunay triangulation is computed using the extracted minutiae features. Next, a robust representation is defined for the fingerprints known as extended triangulation which is a enhanced model of Delaunay triangulation [17]. Finally, the computed extended triangulation is classified such that the retrieval algorithm searches in reduced space of the database. The overview of the indexing framework is shown in Fig. 2.1. Various steps involved in the indexing process are discussed in the following:

2.2.1 Minutiae Extraction

In this work, the minutiae are considered as the key features for the fingerprints. The minutiae points considered are (i) bifurcation points and (ii) end points. A bifurcation point is a point where the ridge forks or diverges into branch ridges. An end point is a point where a ridge ends abruptly. To extract the minutiae features from the fingerprint images, we used the Nuerotechnology VeriFinger SDK [18]. A sample fingerprint and its extracted minutiae are shown in Fig. 2.2 (bifurcation points are represented with circle symbol and end points are represented with square symbol).

Let $p = (x, y, t, \theta)$ be a minutiae feature point of a fingerprint, where (x, y) is its position in the fingerprint, t is its type (fork or end), and θ is its orientation or angle with respect to x-axis. The process of computing the minutiae orientation is shown in Fig. 2.3. The orientation of a minutiae point (either bifurcation or end) is measured by calculating the angle between the tangent to the ridge line at the minutiae position and the x-axis.

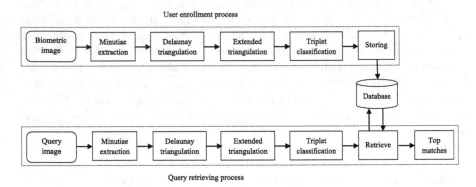

Fig. 2.1 Overview of the proposed approach

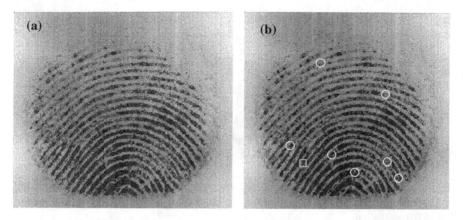

Fig. 2.2 **a** A sample fingerprint **b** Retrieved minutiae (*circle-* bifurcation points; *square-* end points)

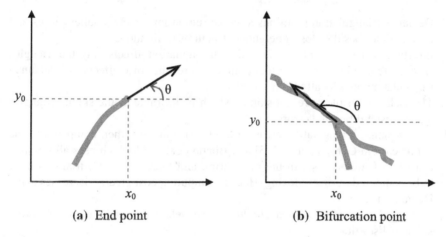

(a) End point **(b)** Bifurcation point

Fig. 2.3 Minutiae position and its orientation extraction process

2.2.2 *Computation of Delaunay Triangulation*

Once the minutiae features have been extracted, their Delaunay triangulation is computed. Let $P = \{p_1, p_2, ..., p_n\}$ be the set of extracted minutiae points from a fingerprint. Then the Delaunay triangulation T of minutiae set P is a maximal planar subdivision in which no edge connecting two vertices can be included to it without destroying its planarity. Delaunay triangle contains no other point of P in its circumcircle. Figure 2.4 shows the Delaunay triangulation of the minutiae for one of the fingerprints. The motivation of using Delaunay triangulation in this work is that the Delaunay triplets possess certain unique properties compared to other topological structures [19–21], including the following:

(a)   **(b)**   **(c)**

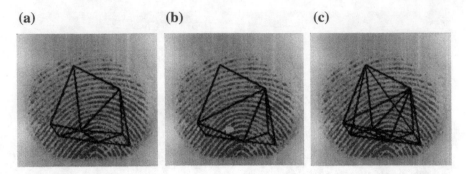

Fig. 2.4 Triangulation for a sample fingerprint [22]: **a** Delaunay triangulation; **b** Structure of the Delaunay triangulation after missing a minutiae point (missing minutiae is shown with star); **c** Extended triangulation

1. Delaunay triangulation partitions a whole region into many smaller pieces and exactly describes the closest neighbor structures of minutiae.
2. Insertion of a new point in a Delaunay triangulation affects only the triangles whose circum circles contain that point. As a result, noise affects the Delaunay triangulation only locally [20];
3. The Delaunay triplets are not skinny which is desirable as the skinny triangles lead to instabilities and errors.
4. The Delaunay triangulation creates only O(n) triangles when compared to the approaches in Germain et al. [15] and Bhanu et al. [16] which uses all possible triangles of minutiae set in the fingerprint, and therefore O(n^3) triangles have to be compared during indexing. Hence, computing cost greatly decreases using Delaunay triangulation.
5. Compared to other topological structures, the Delaunay triangulation is less sensitive to distortion.

However, the noise seriously affects the Delaunay triangulation structure which is a common problem in image processing. Figure 2.4a, b shows one such example with spurious minutiae for two fingerprints of the same user. So, to minimize this, the Delaunay triangulation is enhanced to form a new structure called extended triangulation [17].

2.2.3   Retrieval of Extended Triplet Set

Let T be the Delaunay triangulation of a fingerprint with minutiae set $P = \{p_1, p_2, ..., p_n\}$, and $G = \{P, E\}$ is its Delaunay graph; where E is its edge set. Before defining the extended triangulation of P, let we first explore the triangular hull of a point $p_i \in P$. Let $N_i = \{p_j | (p_i, p_j) \in E\}$ be the set of neighborhood minutiae of p_i in the Delaunay graph G. Then the triangular hull of p_i denoted by

H_i is the Delaunay triangulation of N_i. Now, the extended Delaunay triangulation $S = \{T \cup H_1 \cup H_2 \cup .. \cup H_n\}$ [17]. The extended triangulation for a fingerprint is shown in Fig. 2.4c. It can be seen that the extended triangulation is more robust against distortions. For example, Fig. 2.4a shows the Delaunay triangulation of a fingerprint. Figure 2.4b shows the changes in structure of the triangulation due to missing of a minutiae point. This results in false rejection. However, the extended triangulation (Fig. 2.4c) contains the triangles of both Fig. 2.4a, b. In other words Fig. 2.4c shows T and the triangular hull H_x that is formed when feature x is missed, i.e., $T \cup H_x$. From this example, we can say that, even when the system fails to extract feature x (i.e., missing minutiae) at the time of identification, the corresponding triangles can be found in the extended set and increases the accuracy. Note that this is not possible with Delaunay triangulation. Further, this is also true for fake minutiae [22].

The extended triangulation contains more triangles than Delaunay triangulation, i.e., $|S| \geq |T|$ (Fig. 2.4). But $|S| \in O(n)$ like Delaunay triangulation [17]. The following theorem proves this.

Theorem 1 *The number of triangles in S is O(n) [17].*

Proof The number of triangles in S can be given as follows:

$$|S| \leq |T| + \sum_{i=1}^{n} |H_i|. \tag{2.1}$$

The number of triangles in a Delaunay triangulation T of n points can be bounded by $2n - 1$, i.e., $|T| = 2n - 1$ [17, 19]. This is also true with the case of each triangular hull H_i. So, $|H_i| = 2d_i - 1$, where d_i is degree of the p_i. Hence, Eq. 2.1 can be transformed as follows:

$$|S| \leq (2n - 1) + \sum_{i=1}^{n} (2d_i - 1),$$

$$\leq 2n - 1 + 2 \sum_{i=1}^{n} d_i - n, \tag{2.2}$$

$$\leq n - 1 + 2 \sum_{i=1}^{n} d_i.$$

According to handshaking lemma of graph theory, the sum of the degrees of all the vertices of a graph is equal to twice the number of edges, i.e., $\sum_{i=1}^{n} d_i = 2|E|$ [23]. So, Eq. 2.2 can be transformed as follows:

$$|S| \leq n - 1 + 4|E|. \tag{2.3}$$

Further, according to Euler's formula, the number of edges (E) for a planar graph with vertices $(n) \geq 3$ is less than or equal to $3n - 6$, i.e., $|E| \leq 3n - 6$ [23]. Thus, Eq. 2.3 can be transformed to Eq. 2.4:

$$|S| \leq n - 1 + 4(3n - 6)$$
$$\leq 13n - 25.$$

(2.4)

From Eq. 2.4, we have $|S| \leq 13n - 25$, proving that $|S| \in O(n)$.   □

2.2.4 Hierarchical Decomposition of Extended Set

In the next step, the extended triangles of the fingerprint are classified based on the combination of type of minutiae at the vertices of each triangle. Figure 2.5 shows an example of an extended triangle. Let α_1, α_2, and α_3 are the minimal, medial, and maximal angles in the triangle, respectively. The vertices of the triangle are labeled as V_1, V_2, and V_3 corresponding to the angles α_1, α_2, and α_3. For example, the vertex with α_1 is labeled as V_1. The remaining vertices are labeled accordingly. Then, based on the combination of types of minutiae at the vertices V_1, V_2, and V_3 of the triangle, it is classified into one of eight types as depicted in Table 2.1.

2.2.5 Enrollment

This section explains the process of enrolling (or storing) a fingerprint into an index table. Note that the fingerprint is represented with an extended triangle set S. For each triangle in S, an index X and a feature vector f are computed as shown in Eq. 2.5,

Table 2.1 Hierarchical decomposition of extended triangles

t_c	V_1	V_2	V_3
Triangle class	Minutiae type[a]		
1	b	b	b
2	b	b	e
3	b	e	b
4	b	e	e
5	e	b	b
6	e	b	e
7	e	e	b
8	e	e	e

[a] b-bifurcation point, e-endpoint

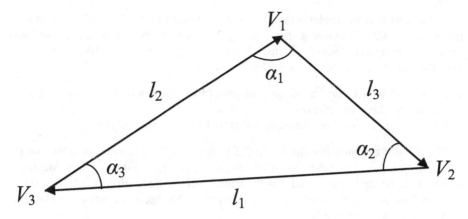

Fig. 2.5 Minutiae triangle

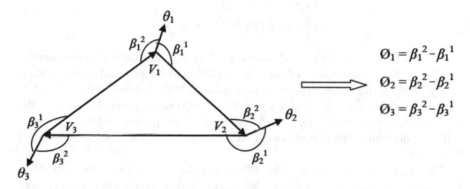

Fig. 2.6 Relative orientation of a minutiae [22]

where t_c is the triangle class, l_1, l_2, l_3 are the lengths of each side of the triangle such that $l_1 \geq l_2 \geq l_3$ and ϕ_1, ϕ_2, ϕ_3 are the relative orientations of minutiae points at vertices V_1, V_2, and V_3, respectively:

$$X = (t_c, \alpha_1, \alpha_2)$$
$$f = (l_1, l_2, l_3, \phi_1, \phi_2, \phi_3). \tag{2.5}$$

The process of computing the relative orientation of a triplet minutiae at vertices (V_i, V_j, V_k) is shown in Fig. 2.6. The relative orientation ϕ_i of minutiae at vertex V_i is defined in Eq. 2.6, where β_i^1 and β_i^2 are the angles that the orientation vector (θ_i) of minutiae at vertex V_i makes with its incident edges, i.e., $V_i V_j$ and $V_i V_k$:

$$\phi_i = \beta_i^1 - \beta_i^2. \tag{2.6}$$

In the next step, the triplet is enrolled into a 3D index table ($ISPACE$) using its index X. The 3D index table is shown in Fig. 2.7a. The index table size is chosen as $max(t_c) \times max(\alpha_1) \times max(\alpha_2)$ bins, where $1 \leq t_c \leq 8$, $0 \leq \alpha_1 \leq 180$, $0 \leq \alpha_2 \leq 180$. Further, it can be seen that each bin has two lists:

- $I_{id}List$—This list stores the fingerprint ids of the triplets which are mapped (i.e., indexed) to this particular bin;
- $FVList$—This list stores the feature vectors of the mapped triplets.

Enrolling of a triangle into the $ISPACE$ is shown in Eq. 2.7, where X is the index space location (i.e., bin) where the triplet to enroll; I_{id} represents the image identity to which the triplet belongs; and f is the feature vector of the triplet [22]. Note that the first dimension (say triplet class) partitions the 3D index space into eight classes (2D tables). This is shown in Fig. 2.7a:

$$ISPACE[X].I_{id}List \leftarrow I_{id}$$
$$ISPACE[X].FVList \leftarrow f. \tag{2.7}$$

The process of enrolling a triplet into the $ISPACE$ is illustrated with an example: Let $X = (4, 50, 65)$ be the index of one of the triplets of an image x and f be its feature vector. Using X, the indexing algorithm access the (4,50,65)th bin of the $ISPACE$ and places x and f at the $I_{id}List$ and $FVList$ of it respectively. In other words, the algorithm maps to the $(50, 65)$th location in the 4th partition of the $ISPACE$ and store the triplet's feature vector f and its image identity x in the lists provided (Fig. 2.7b).

The remaining triangles in extended set are also enrolled into the $ISPACE$ likewise. We repeat this process for other fingerprints in the database. Finally, note that more than one triangle may map to the same bin of $ISPACE$ because different triangles may have same index. In other words, some bins of the $ISPACE$ may receive multiple triangles. Hence, the insertion of image identity I_{id} along with the feature vector f into the $ISPACE$ helps to eliminate the false matches. The indexing mechanism is given in Algorithm 2.1.

Algorithm 2.1 Indexing: Fingerprint enrollment into the index space

---
1: **INPUT:** x: Input fingerprint, S: Extended triplet set of x, and $ISPACE$: Index space.
2: **OUTPUT:** A: Updated $ISPACE$.
3: **for** each extended triplet of fingerprint x **do**
4:    $t_c \leftarrow i$,   where $1 \leq i \leq 8$.   // Compute the triplet's class t_c
5:    $f \leftarrow (l_1, l_2, l_3, \phi_1, \phi_2, \phi_3)$.   // Compute triplet's feature vector f
6:    $X \leftarrow (t_c, \alpha_1, \alpha_2)$.   //$X$ is triplet's index in $ISPACE$
7:    $ISPACE[X].I_{id}List \leftarrow x$.
8:    $ISPACE[X].FVList \leftarrow f$
9: **end for**
10: **RETURN** Updated $ISPACE$

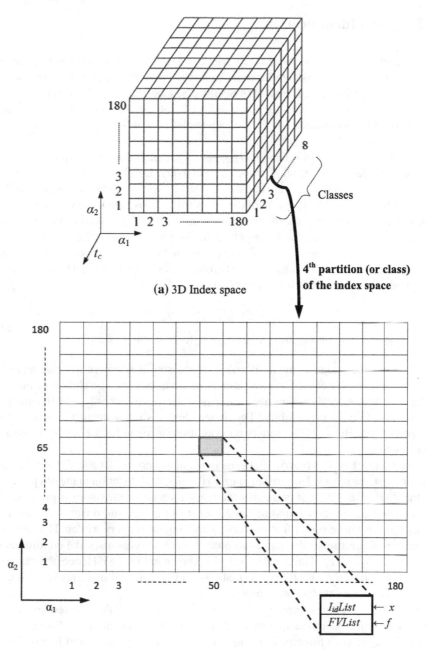

(a) 3D Index space

4th **partition (or class)**
of the index space

(b) One sample partition (let say fourth) of the index space

Fig. 2.7 a Proposed 3D Index space ($ISPACE$) structure, **b** Process of enrolling a triplet into the $ISPACE$: A triplet with index $(4, 50, 65)$ is stored into the $(50, 65)$th location (shown with color) of the 4th partition in the $ISPACE$, where f is the feature vector of the triplet and x is its image identity

2.3 Query Identification

Query identification is the process of retrieving a small set of candidates C from the $ISPACE$ which are most similar to it. To do this, first, the extended triangle set of the query is computed as discussed in Sect. 2.2.3. Then, the triangles in the retrieved extended set are classified as discussed in Sect. 2.2.4. Let a query fingerprint consist of n triplets in its extended set S. For each triplet in S, its index and feature vector are computed.

Let $X = (t_c, \alpha_1, \alpha_2)$, $f = (l_1, l_2, l_3, \phi_1, \phi_2, \phi_3)$, and t_c be the index, feature vector, and class of a enrolled triplet, respectively. Let $X' = (t'_c, \alpha'_1, \alpha'_2)$, $f' = (l'_1, l'_2, l'_3, \phi'_1, \phi'_2, \phi'_3)$ and t'_c be the index, feature vector, and class of a enrolled triplet, respectively. The index X' of the query triplet is used to access the $ISPACE$ and retrieve a set of fingerprints from the $I_{id}List$ of that bin, whose triplet feature vectors satisfy the set of conditions given in Eq. 2.8 as successful correspondences to the query triplet, where T_l and T_ϕ are predefined thresholds. In other words, two triangles are said to be matched, iff their feature vectors are similar. Let these retrieved image identities are stored into a temporary list L:

$$|l_1 - l'_1|, |l_2 - l'_2|, |l_3 - l'_3| < T_l,$$
$$and \quad |\phi_1 - \phi^1_1|, |\phi_2 - \phi^1_2|, |\phi_3 - \phi^1_3| < T_\phi. \tag{2.8}$$

Note that the image acquisition and preprocessing is sensitive to noise and distortions, and the features of the two images of same user may be shifted or missed. Therefore, the retrieval systems need to consider the triplets not only from the mapped bin but also from its nearest bins. The image identities in the nearest bins (i.e., predefined neighborhood λ) that satisfy the conditions given in Eq. 2.8 are retrieved and stored into L.

Illustration: Let $X' = (6, 65, 40)$ be the index of a query triplet and f' be its feature vector. First, the retrieval algorithm maps to the (65,40)th location in the 6th partition of the $ISPACE$. Then, it compares the feature vector of the query triplet, i.e., f' with each feature vector found in the $FVList$ of the bin, and retrieves all the I_{id}s from $I_{id}List$ whose triplet feature vectors are similar to query triplet. The retrieval algorithm also retrieves the I_{id}s from predefined λ which satisfy the conditions in Eq. 2.8. Let $\lambda = 1$, i.e., window size is 3×3 (shown in Fig. 2.8). Hence, the range of locations is from (64, 39) to (66, 41) (shown in Fig. 2.8). All these retrieved image identities (I_{id}s) are stored into temporary list L.

Similarly, this process is repeated for each query triplet and the selected fingerprint ids I_{id}s are retrieved into temporary list L. In the next step, the number of occurrences (i.e., $Votes$) of each fingerprint identity, i.e., I_{id} in L, is counted and forms the set as $\{(I_{id}, Votes_{I_{id}})\}$, where I_{id} is the image identity and $Votes_{I_{id}}$ is the number of occurrences of I_{id} in L. Finally, the I_{id}s whose $Votescore$ greater than a threshold (T) are retrieved as similar fingerprints (i.e., candidate set C) to the query. The vote

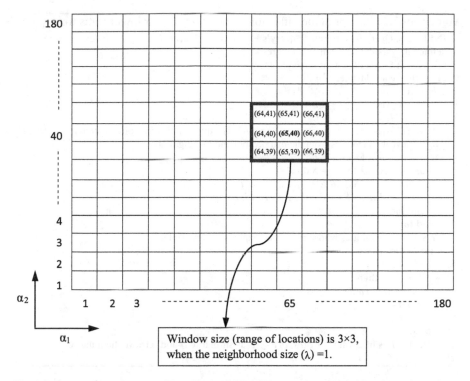

Fig. 2.8 Range of locations considered in the $ISPACE$, to retrieve the similar triplets for a query triplet

score of an image identity represented as $Votescore_{I_{id}}$ is defined in Eq. 2.9, where $Votes_{I_{id}}$ is the number of corresponding matched triangles between q and I_{td}, and n is the number of query triangles. The retrieval method is given in Algorithm 2.2:

$$Votescore_{I_{id}} = \left(\frac{Votes_{I_{id}}}{n}\right) \times 100. \tag{2.9}$$

2.4 Experimental Results

To study the effectiveness of the proposed indexing approach, a number of experiments have been conducted on FVC fingerprint databases. This section describes the experiments carried out and the results observed.

Algorithm 2.2 Fingerprint identification: Retrieving similar fingerprints for a query

---

1: **INPUT:** q: Query fingerprint, S: query's Extended triplet set, $ISPACE$: Index space, λ: predefined neighborhood, T: matching threshold

2: **OUTPUT:** C: Set of similar fingerprints.

3: **for** each extended triplet of q **do**

4:　　$F \leftarrow \{\}, Im \leftarrow \{\}$

5:　　$t_c \leftarrow i$,　where $1 \leq i \leq 8$.

6:　　$f \leftarrow (l_1, l_2, l_3, \phi_1, \phi_2, \phi_3)$.

7:　　$X \leftarrow (t_c, \alpha_1, \alpha_2)$.　　　　　　　　　//$X$ is triplet's index i.e., bin location in $ISPACE$

　　　// Retrieve the identities from the mapped bin and its neighbors

8:　　**for** $j = \alpha_1 - \lambda$ to $\alpha_1 + \lambda$ **do**

9:　　　**for** $k = \alpha_2 - \lambda$ to $\alpha_2 + \lambda$ **do**

10:　　　　$F \leftarrow F \cup ISPACE[t_c, j, k].FVList$

11:　　　　$Im \leftarrow Im \cup ISPACE[t_c, j, k].I_{id}List$

12:　　　**end for**

13:　　**end for**

　　　// Select the identities whose triplets are equal to query triplet

14:　　**for** l=1 to $|F|$ **do**

15:　　　$f' \leftarrow F.l$

16:　　　**if** $f' \cong f$ **then**

17:　　　　$L \leftarrow L \cup Im.l$.

18:　　　**end if**

19:　　**end for**

20: **end for**

21: Select the I_{id}s in L whose $Votescore \geq T$ as similar to q and retrieve them into C.

22: **RETURN** C

2.4.1 Parameter Selection

Selection of appropriate values for different parameters involved in the system is critical for achieving its best performance. One such important parameter is the selection of neighborhood size (λ) (Sect. 3.3). By fixing the matching threshold T, an experiment is conducted with various λ sizes starting from 0 to 6, and the corresponding MR and PR are recorded for every λ (Table 2.2). The relationship between MR, PR, and λ is shown in Figs. 2.9 and 2.10 for FVC 2002 and FVC 2004 fingerprint databases, respectively. It is observed that the PR increases with the λ while MR decreases. But for a real-time application, both MR and PR should be low. Hence, an optimal value for the λ should be chosen such that the system achieves low MR as well as low PR. Therefore, the optimum λ value is chosen as where the two curves intersects, i.e., MR = PR.

In the experiment, for FVC 2002 DB1 and FVC 2004 DB4 databases, the optimum λ size obtained is in and around 3 (i.e., window size is 7×7). For FVC 2002 DB2, FVC 2002 DB3, FVC 2004 DB1, and FVC 2004 DB2, the optimum λ value is in and around 4 (i.e., window size is 9×9). In case of FVC 2002 DB4, the optimum λ value is 5 (i.e., window size is 11×11). Table 2.3 shows the optimum λ value obtained for different databases.

Table 2.2 Effect of neighborhood size on the indexing performance

λ	2002DB1		2002DB2		2002DB3		2002DB4		2004DB1		2004DB2		2004DB4	
	MR	PR	MR	PR	MR	PR	MR	PR	MR	PR	MR	PR	MR	PR
0	28.45	10.23	32.14	14.23	45.42	15.93	45.56	9.81	42.54	12.69	32.17	8.86	26.65	9.89
1	26.12	10.54	31.05	15.23	40.52	16.26	39.42	12.65	40.15	14.32	29.47	11.26	24.42	9.51
2	20.08	12.75	28.26	17.45	37.19	17.64	34.18	15.26	35.48	16.54	24.20	12.13	17.26	10.87
3	**15.11**	**14.42**	26.11	20.92	32.15	19.05	32.45	20.32	28.65	19.09	19.87	15.04	**13.42**	**12.86**
4	11.32	16.55	**24.21**	**23.98**	**24.69**	**23.18**	28.96	24.58	**23.09**	**21.86**	**16.91**	**18.82**	10.68	15.26
5	8.26	19.36	23.65	26.09	20.54	29.04	**26.35**	**27.28**	17.08	26.40	16.08	20.15	9.86	19.04
6	5.32	20.89	23.03	27.68	18.23	35.45	25.24	28.86	12.75	30.24	15.32	21.86	9.12	21.31

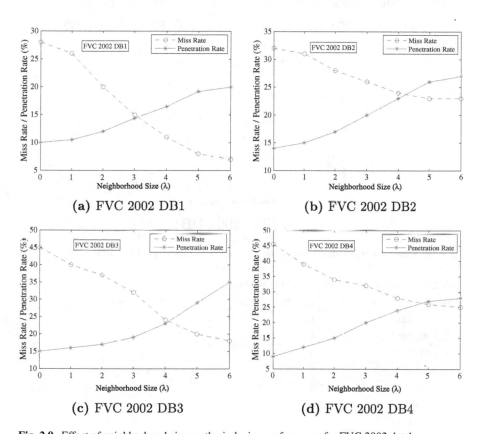

(a) FVC 2002 DB1

(b) FVC 2002 DB2

(c) FVC 2002 DB3

(d) FVC 2002 DB4

Fig. 2.9 Effect of neighborhood size on the indexing performance for FVC 2002 databases

2.4.2 Results

Once the optimum λ value is chosen, an experiment was conducted to evaluate the performance of the proposed indexing technique for different databases. At various threshold (T) values, we determine the MR and PR of the system. The relationship

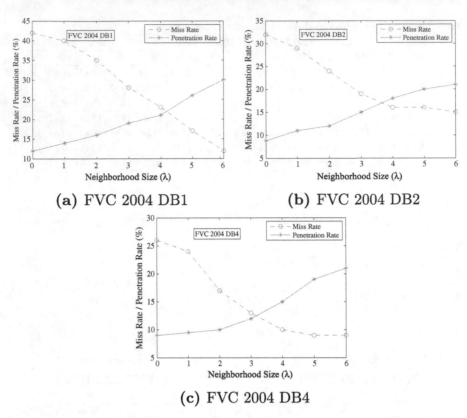

Fig. 2.10 Effect of neighborhood size on the indexing performance for FVC 2004 databases

Table 2.3 Optimum neighborhood size (λ) obtained for different databases

Database	Optimum λ value	Window size
FVC 2002 DB1	3	7×7
FVC 2002 DB2	4	9×9
FVC 2002 DB3	4	9×9
FVC 2002 DB4	5	11×11
FVC 2004 DB1	4	9×9
FVC 2004 DB2	4	9×9
FVC 2002 DB4	3	7×7

between MR, PR, and T is plotted in Figs. 2.11 and 2.12 for FVC 2002 and FVC 2004 fingerprint databases, respectively. It is observed that, for small values of T, MR is low and PR is high which is not desirable. On the other hand, increasing the T value decreases the PR but it increases the MR, which is also not desirable. High PR

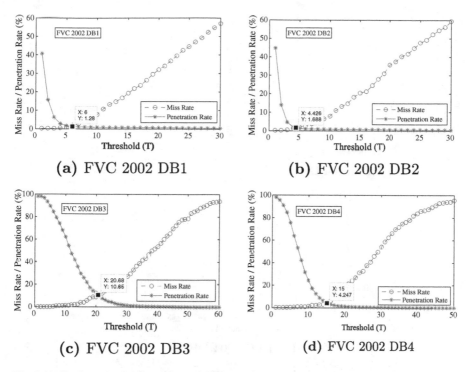

Fig. 2.11 Performance of the proposed indexing approach on FVC 2002 databases

results in more search time, while high MR results in a less secure system. However, as noted earlier, an effective identification system should have low MR as well as PR. Hence, the performance of the system at MR = PR is recorded (Figs. 2.11 and 2.12).

It is observed that, for FVC 2002 DB1, at $MR = PR$, the system achieves a PR and MR of 1.28%. In other words, the system searches only 1.28% of the database and genuine image is identified (i.e., HR) with an accuracy of 98.72% (i.e., 100–1.28%). Further, the system achieves a PR and MR of 1.68, 10.65, 4.24, 9.7, 6.55 and 9.47% for FVC 2002 DB2, FVC 2002 DB3, FVC 2002 DB4, FVC 2004 DB1, FVC 2004 DB2, and FVC 2004 DB4 databases, respectively. The PR and HR of the proposed system at $MR = PR$ are shown in Table 2.4 for different databases.

2.4.3   Comparison with Other Related Approaches

In the next experiment, we compared the performance of the proposed approach with Delaunay triplets [20] and Extended triplet approaches [17]. Figures 2.13 and 2.14

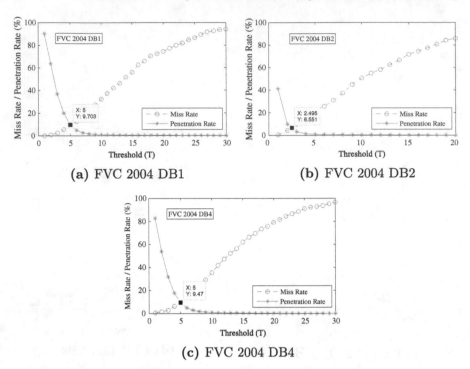

(a) FVC 2004 DB1   (b) FVC 2004 DB2

(c) FVC 2004 DB4

Fig. 2.12 Performance of the proposed indexing approach on FVC 2004 databases

Table 2.4 PR and HR (i.e., $HR = 100 - MR$) of the proposed system at $MR = PR$ for different databases

Database	PR(%)	HR(%)
FVC 2002 DB1	1.28	98.72
FVC 2002 DB2	1.68	98.32
FVC 2002 DB3	10.65	89.35
FVC 2002 DB4	4.24	95.76
FVC 2004 DB1	9.7	90.3
FVC 2004 DB2	6.55	93.45
FVC 2002 DB4	9.47	90.53

show the results of different approaches on FVC 2002 and FVC 2004, respectively. The PR of the proposed approach is less compared to Delaunay and extended triangulation-based approaches for most of the datasets. This shows that the partitioning of the index space results in reducing the search space during identification.

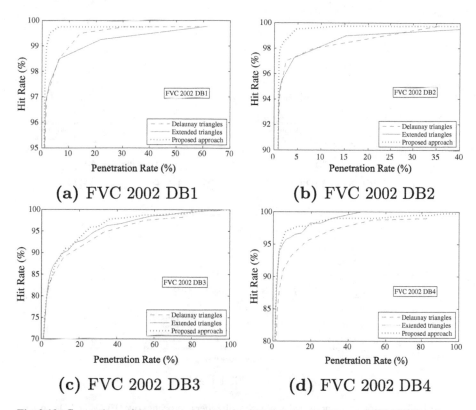

Fig. 2.13 Comparison of the proposed approach with other approaches over FVC 2002 Databases

2.4.4 Retrieval Time

We analyze the retrieval time of the proposed approach with big-O notation. Let n be the number of triplets in the extended set of query image q; and N be the number of images in the database. Note that $n \ll N$, as seen from Algorithm 2.2, for a given query triplet t:

- First, we compute its class t_c, its feature vector f, and its index X. Note that each of these takes $O(1)$ time.
- Next, we retrieve all the I_{id}s from $I_{id}Lists$ corresponding to the bins from $X - \lambda$ to $X + \lambda$ into a set named "Im". This process takes $O(1)$ time.
- Then, a set of I_{id}s are retrieved from the Im into a temporary list L, whose triplet feature vectors are similar to query triplet feature vector. Let m be the size of the Im. This process requires $O(m)$ time. Note that $m \ll N$.

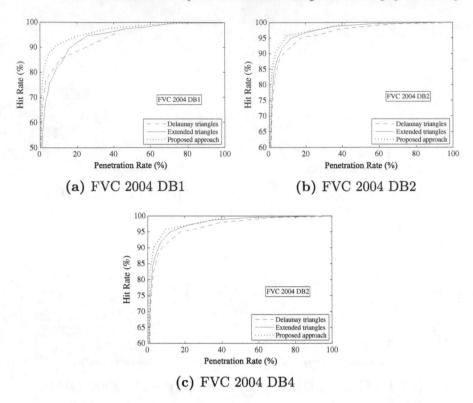

(a) FVC 2004 DB1   (b) FVC 2004 DB2

(c) FVC 2004 DB4

Fig. 2.14 Comparison of the proposed approach with other approaches over FVC 2004 Databases

Hence, the total time required for each query triplet to retrieve the I_{id}s from the index space into the temporary list L is $O(m)$ time. Note that there are n triplets in the extended set of the query image. So, this retrieval process takes $O(nm)$ time.

Finally, we count the number of occurrences of each I_{id} in L and select top-ranked ones into a candidate set C. Let the size of L is p, where $p \ll N$. This process requires $O(p)$ time. Hence, the total retrieval time for a query image can be approximated as $O(nm) + O(p)$.

2.5   Summary

In this chapter, an efficient indexing algorithm using hierarchical decomposition of extended triplets is proposed. It has been shown that the proposed algorithm performs better for the fingerprint databases. The decomposition of extended triplets provides better classification in the database, and further reduces search space. Without increasing the computing cost, the extended triangulation reduces the search space and increases the response time as it produces only O(n) triplets. Further, this new representation is more robust against distortions compared to all other structures.

References

1. AADHAAR. **Unique Identification Authority of India**. http://uidai.gov.in/, July 2014.
2. **Singapore Immigration and Checkpoint authority**. http://www.ica.gov.sg/page.aspx? pageid=407, september 2014.
3. CROSSING U.S. BORDERS. http://www.dhs.gov/crossing-us-borders, July 2014.
4. FIND BIOMETRICS. **Mobile Biometrics, PDAs & Laptop Fingerprint Readers**. http:// findbiometrics.com/applications/mobile-biometrics/, september 2014.
5. PLANET BIOMETRICS. **Physical Access and Attendence**. http://www.planetbiometrics.com/ physical-access/, september 2014.
6. **Iris Scans at Amsterdam Airport Schiphol**. http://www.schiphol.nl/Travellers/AtSchiphol/ Privium/Privium/IrisScans.htm, september 2014.
7. **United Arab Emirates Deployment of Iris Recognition:**. http://www.cl.cam.ac.uk/jgd1000/ deployments.html, July 2014.
8. TSA. **Transportation Security Administration**. http://www.tsa.gov/, september 2014.
9. J. HAMMOND. **Biometric traveler screening introduced in Orlando, Denver next**. http:// www.examiner.com/article/biometric-traveler-screening-introduced-orlando-denver-next/, september 2014.
10. R. BORO AND S.D. ROY. **Fast and Robust Projective Matching for Fingerprints Using Geometric Hashing**. In *Indian Conference on Computer Vision, Graphics and Image Processing*, pages 681–688, 2004.
11. Y. LAMDAN AND H.J. WOLFSON. **Geometric hashing: A general and efficient model-based recognition scheme**. In *ICCV*, **88**, pages 238–249, 1988.
12. H. MEHROTRA, B. MAJHI, AND P. GUPTA. **Robust iris indexing scheme using geometric hashing of SIFT keypoints**. *Journal of Network and Computer Applications*, **33**(3):300–313, 2010.
13. D.G. LOWE. **Distinctive Image Features from Scale-Invariant Keypoints**. *International Journal of Computer Vision*, **60**(2):91–110, 2004.
14. SIFT. **SIFT for matlab:**. http://www.vlfeat.org/vedaldi/code/sift.html.
15. R.S. GERMAIN, A. CALIFANO, AND S. COLVILLE. **Fingerprint Matching Using Transformation Parameter Clustering**. *IEEE Computing in Science and Engineering*, **4**(4):42–49, 1997.
16. B. BHANU AND X. TAN. **Fingerprint indexing based on novel features of minutiae triplets**. *IEEE Transactions on Pattern Analysis and Machine Intelligence*, **25**(5):616–622, 2003.
17. A.G. ALONSO, J.H. PALANCAR, E.R. REINA, AND A.M. BRISEÑO. **Indexing and retrieving in fingerprint databases under structural distortions**. *Expert Systems with Applications*, **40**(8):2858–2871, 2013.
18. "NEUROTECHNOLOGY". **VeriFinger SDK**. http://www.neurotechnology.com/verifinger.html, January 2014.
19. M.D. BERG, M.V. KREVELD, M. OVERMARS, AND O.C. SCHWARZKOPF. *Computational geometry*. Springer, 2000.
20. G. BEBIS, T. DEACONU, AND M. GEORGIOPOULOS. **Fingerprint Identification Using Delaunay Triangulation**. In *International Conference on Information, Intelligence, and Systems*, pages 452–452, 1999.
21. ILAIAH KAVATI, MUNAGA VNK PRASAD, AND CHAKRAVARTHY BHAGVATI. **Vein Pattern Indexing Using Texture and Hierarchical Decomposition of Delaunay Triangulation**. *Security in Computing and Communications*, pages 213–222, 2013.

22. ILAIAH   KAVATI,   VAMSHIKRISHNA   CHENNA,   MUNAGA   VNK   PRASAD,   AND
    CHAKRAVARTHY   BHAGVATI. **Classification of extended delaunay triangulation for fin-
    gerprint indexing**. In *Modelling Symposium (AMS), 2014 8th Asia*, pages 153–158. IEEE,
    2014.
23. N. BIGGS, E.K. LLOYD, AND R.J. WILSON. *Graph Theory, 1736-1936*. Clarendon Press,
    1986.

Chapter 3
Efficient Score-Based Indexing Technique for Fast Palmprint Retrieval

Abstract Biometric identification systems capture biometric (i.e., fingerprint, palm, and iris) images and store them in a central database. During identification, the query biometric image is compared against all images in the central database. Typically, this exhaustive matching process (linear search) works very well for the small databases. However, biometric databases are usually huge and this process increases the response time of the identification system. To address this problem, we present an efficient technique that computes a fixed-length index code for each biometric image. Further, an index table is created based on the indices of all individuals. During identification, a set of candidate images which are similar to the query are retrieved from the index table based on the values of query index using voting scheme that takes less time. The technique has been tested on benchmark PolyU palmprint database and the results show a better performance in terms of response time and search speed compared to the state-of-the-art indexing methods.

Keywords Index code · Palmprint · SIFT · Sample images · Match scores

3.1 Introduction

This chapter presents a score-based indexing approach for the palmprints. The first such attempt was made by Maeda et al. [1]. They compute a match score vector for each image by comparing it against all the database images and stored these vectors permanently as a matrix. Though, the approach achieves quicker response time, it takes linear time in worst case and also storing of match score matrix leads to increase in the space complexity. Gyaourova et al. [2] improved the work on match scores by choosing a small set of reference images from the database. For every image in the database, a match score vector (index code) was computed by matching it against the sample set using a matcher and stored this match score vector as a row in an index table. However, a sequential search is done in the index space for identification of best matches which takes linear time and is prohibitive for a database containing millions of images. Paliwal et al. [3], used vector approximation (VA+) file to store the match score vectors and k-NN search, palmprint texture to retrieve best matches. However,

© The Author(s) 2017   41
I. Kavati et al., *Efficient Biometric Indexing and Retrieval Techniques for Large-Scale Systems*, SpringerBriefs in Computer Science, DOI 10.1007/978-3-319-57660-2_3

the performance of VA+ file method generally degrades as dimensionality increases [4]. This chapter presents an indexing method that computes a fixed-length index code for each input biometric image based on match scores. The method proposes an efficient storing and searching method for the biometric database using these index codes. The proposed searching technique avoids the sequential scan on the database for identification and uses voting scheme, which results in a rapid search that takes less time.

3.2 Indexing

This section discusses our proposed methodology for indexing the biometric databases. The concept behind this approach is that if two palmprints p and q belong to same user, then their match scores (keys) against a third image (let s) are almost equal. This enables us to use these scores as index keys for the palmprints in an index table and arrange them like traditional records. To indentify a query palmprint, we compute its key (i.e., its match score with s) and retrieve the palmprint that have same key in the index table. However, many palmprints may have same key (i.e., match score against s) and mapped to the same bin of the index table. For example, alphabets X and Z are different but have same distance (score) to Y. This is shown in Table 3.1. Hence, a set of palmprints are retrieved as similar to the query palmprint. This retrieved set contains few palmprints that are not similar to q but have same score against s. Hence, multiple samples can be used to filter out these false matches. An overview of our proposed technique is shown in Fig. 3.1. The different steps involved in our approach are discussed in the following.

	Score (or Key)	List of Palmprints
Table 3.1 Palmprints are arranged in ascending order of their scores against sample palmprint	0	$PList$
	1	$PList$
	2	$PList$
	–	–
	–	–
	$x-1$	$PList$
	x	$PList$
	$x+1$	$PList$
	–	–
	–	–
	100	$PList$

User enrollment process

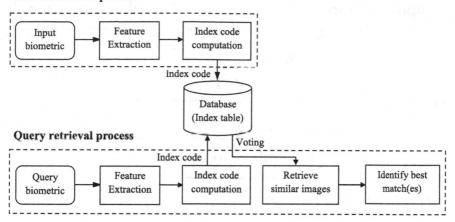

Fig. 3.1 Overview of the proposed approach

3.2.1 Feature Extraction

This section describes the key features used for the palmprint images. In this work, we use scale invariant feature transform (SIFT) points as the key features [5–8].

3.2.2 Index Code Computation

This section proposes an efficient method to compute indexes for biometric images that makes use of a sample image set. The index code computation process is shown in Fig. 3.2. An input image is compared against a set of sample images; the resultant set of match scores (i.e., keys) is called the index code (i.e., $INDEX$) of the input image [2].

This can be formulated as follows: Let a be an input image and $S = \{s_1, s_2, \ldots, s_k\}$ be the selected sample image set. Then, the index code of image a represented by $INDEX_a$ is given in Eq. 3.1, where $m(a, s_i)$ is the match score (i.e., key) of image a against i^{th} sample image.

$$INDEX_a = \{m(a, s_1), m(a, s_2), \ldots, m(a, s_k)\}$$
$$= \{key_1, key_2, \ldots, key_k\} \tag{3.1}$$

The match score between two images is computed by comparing their key features in Euclidean space [9]. Note that $INDEX_a$ is the index code of image a and consists of k keys.

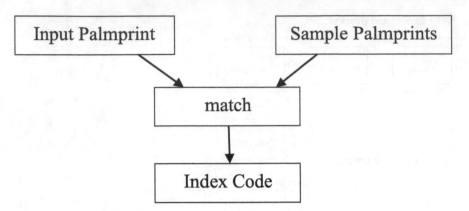

Fig. 3.2 Index code computation process

3.2.3   *Index Table Creation and User Enrolment*

To enroll the palmprints, a 2D Index Table A of size $100 \times k$ is created. Each column of the table corresponds to one sample image in the sample set. The match scores obtained are normalized in the range 0-100. For a given palmprint a, we compute the index code which consists of k keys. Let $x = m(a, s_i)$ be the key_i of palmprint a against sample image s_i. Then palmprint a is enrolled into bin $A(x, s_i)$. This process is repeated with other keys of palmprint a and is enrolled to the corresponding bin of the index table. The index table organization is shown in Table 3.2. It can be seen that each bin of the table $A(x, s_i)$ contains a list of palmprints (i.e., PList), whose match score is x against sample image s_i.

Table 3.2   Index table consists of $k + 1$ columns where the first column is the key and remaining k columns are corresponding to one palmprint of the sample set

Score (or Key)	s_1	s_2	–	s_k
0	PList	PList	–	PList
1	PList	PList	–	PList
2	PList	PList	–	PList
–	–	–	–	–
–	–	–	–	–
$x - 1$	PList	PList	–	PList
x	PList	PList	–	PList
$x + 1$	PList	PList	–	PList
–	–	–	–	–
–	–	–	–	–
100	PList	PList	–	PList

We illustrate the palmprint enrollment process with an example. Let $S =$ $\{s_1, s_2, s_3\}$ be a sample set of three palmprints (i.e., $k = 3$). Thus, the index code of a palmprint consists of three keys each against one sample image. Hence, the index table requires three columns. Let a be an input palmprint and $\{45, 59, 35\}$ be its index code. We use the first key, i.e., 45 and enroll a into (45, 1) location in the index table A. Then, using the second key 59, we access $A(59, 2)$ bin and enroll the palmprint identity a into the $PList$. Finally, using third key 35, we enroll a into $PList$ at $A(35, 3)$ of index table. The other palmprints of the database are also enrolled into the index table likewise. Finally, each column of the index table contains all palmprints in the order of their keys against corresponding sample image (Table 3.2). Algorithm 3.1 explains the process of enrolling a palmprint into index table.

Algorithm 3.1 Palmprint enrollment process

1: **INPUT:** Input Palmprint a, Sample image set $S = \{s_1, s_2, .., s_k\}$, Index Table $A(100 \times k)$.
2: **OUTPUT:** Updated A
    // Enroll Palmprint a into A
3: **for** each $s_i \in S$ **do**
4:    $x \leftarrow m(a, s_i)$ // $m(a, s_i)$ is the match score (i.e., key) of a against s_i
5:    $A(x, i).PList \leftarrow a$ //Enroll a into $PList$ at location (x, i) of A.
6: **end for**
7: **RETURN** Updated A.

3.3 Retrieval of Best Matches for a Query

This section proposes an efficient retrieval system to identify a query image from the index table. During identification, the technique retrieves a set of palmprint identities (i.e., candidate list) from the index table which are most similar to the query using voting method. To do this, we first compute the index code of the query. The index code of query image q represented as $INDEX_q$ is given in Eq. 3.2.

$$INDEX_q = \{m(q, s_1), m(q, s_2), \ldots, m(q, s_i), \ldots, m(q, s_k)\} \qquad (3.2)$$

Let $x = m(q, s_i)$ be the ith match score value of the query index code, the algorithm uses x as key to the index table and retrieves all the palmprints ($PList$) found in the bin $A(x, i)$. We also retrieve palmprints from the predefined neighborhood λ of the selected bin in the corresponding column i to handle the natural distortions. Finally, we give a vote to each retrieved image. We repeat this process with other keys of the query index code. In our next step, we accumulate and count the number of votes of each palmprint identity. Finally, we sort all the individuals in descending order based on the number of votes received. We select the individuals whose vote score is greater than a predefined threshold as best matches (candidate list) to the query image.

The query identification process can be illustrated using an example. Let q be a query palmprint and $INDEX_q = \{35, 54, 56\}$. We use key_1 which is 35 to access 35th bin in first column of index table (i.e., $A(35, 1)$) and retrieve all the palmprints found there. Next we also retrieve palmprints from a predefined neighborhood λ. Let $\lambda = 2$. Hence, the range of locations is from 33 $(35 - \lambda)$ to 37 $(35 + \lambda)$ in column 1. We add all these palmprints from locations 33 to 37 into temporary list L. Then, using key_2, we access $A(54, 2)$ and retrieve the palmprints from bins 52 to 56 into L. Further, using key_3, we access $A(56, 3)$ and retrieve the palmprints from bins 54 to 58 into L. Finally, we select the palmprints that have appeared more number of times (receives more votes) than a predefined threshold as potential candidates to q.

The motivation to this voting mechanism is that, if two palmprints (say query and an enrolled palmprint) belong to the same hand, then their scores against a sample palmprint are similar. So the assumption is that, if the database contains the query palmprint identity, the total number of votes received for this is more than other enrolled palmprints.

Algorithm 3.2 Palmprint identification: Retrieving the best match for a query

---

1: **INPUT:** Query Palmprint q, Sample image set $S = \{s_1, s_2, .., s_k\}$, Index Table $A(100 \times k)$, Predefined neighborhood λ.

2: **OUTPUT:** Candidate Set C

  //Retrieve set of similar palmprints to q from A

3: $L \leftarrow \{ \}$

4: **for** each $s_i \in S$ **do**

5:   $x \leftarrow m(q, s_i)$ // $m(q, s_i)$ is the key of q against s_i

6:   **for** $j = x - \lambda$ to $x + \lambda$ **do**

7:     $L \leftarrow L \cup A(j, i).PList$ // L is a temporary list.

8:   **end for**

9: **end for**

10: Retrieve the $P_{id}s$ in L whose Vote score greater than a predefined threshold T as similar to q and retrieve them into C.

11: **RETURN** Candidate Set C.

3.4   Selection of Sample Images

The selection of sample images from the database plays a crucial role in the performance of the system. Images which are more different from one another and represent the qualities of the entire database should be selected as sample images. The sample images should be selected such that they are having distinct characteristics and provide enough information about the database for identification with minimal computational cost [3]. In this work, we explore two different methods for selection of representative images: (a) Max-variance method, (b) k-means clustering.

Let D be the database corresponding to n users. We divided the database into two datasets: *Gallery* (i.e., Training) set consists of M images and *Probe* (i.e., Testing) set consists of N images. For each image in $Gallery$, determine its variance of grayscale intensity values. Let $Gallery = \{U_1, U_2, \ldots, U_n\}$, where U_i is a set of images of subject i. From each set U_i, select one image which is having maximum variance in the set (i.e., the image of better quality). Let $A = \{a_1, a_2, \ldots, a_n\}$ be the set of all selected images. The set A contains the candidates from which sample image set $S = \{s_1, s_2, \ldots, s_k\}$ is selected where $S \subset A$, and $|S| \ll |A|$.

3.4.1 Max-variance Method

The max-variance method sorts the images in set A in descending order based on the variance and selects the top k images (k is determined empirically) for the representative image set S. The idea behind choosing such representative set is that the highly variant images contain significant properties that represent the various qualities of the database.

3.4.2 k-Means Clustering

The second method relies on the concept of clustering. This method partitions the set X into k clusters based on variance using k-means clustering such that images in the same cluster are similar to each other; whereas images in different clusters are dissimilar. As each cluster contains similar images, one image from each cluster which is closer to the cluster centroid is selected for set S as sample of that cluster. Unlike the max-variance method which selects sample images from a single group (i.e., the images with maximum variances), the clustering method selects images from different groups and thus satisfies the aforementioned property.

3.5 Experimental Results

This section shows the performance of the proposed indexing approach experimentally. The experiments are conducted on PolyU palmprint database [10].

First, we validate different parameters such as neighborhood size (λ), selection rules for the sample palmprints, etc., that are involved in this work.

3.5.1 Neighborhood Size (λ)

The neighborhood size λ plays a major role on the system performance. An experiment is conducted by varying the λ values from 0 to 8 and observed the system miss

Table 3.3 Effect of neighborhood size λ on indexing performance

λ	MR	PR
0	55.63	12.42
1	52.46	14.56
2	48.53	16.19
3	38.62	18.55
4	33.06	20.62
5	**30.03**	**26.82**
6	27.52	33.91
7	20.13	35.77
8	12.28	38.06

rate (MR) and penetration rate (PR). This is shown in Table 3.3. It is observed that, the PR increases with λ while MR decreases. Hence, the optimum value for the λ is chosen as a point where the MR and PR values are approximately equal which is 5.

3.5.2 Selection Rules for Sample Palmprints

The sample images should be very different from another and represent entire qualities of the database. Hence, an experiment is conducted to validate the system performance using various rules for the selection of sample images. Four different selection rules are considered (Fig. 3.3):

1. Max-variance approach
2. k-means approach
3. Randomly selected k palmprints
4. First k palmprints of the database

The proposed max-variance and k-means algorithms achieve less PR and high HR compared to other approaches. This performance (Fig. 3.3) shows the superiority of proposed rules for the selection of sample palmprints. Further, it can be observed that the proposed k-means clustering rule performs better than the max-variance method. This shows the ability of the k-means clustering approach for retrieving the sample palmprints from the database.

3.5.3 Results and Performance Comparison

This section describes the results of the proposed approach and its comparison with the prominent approaches in the literature. The HR and PR of the system at various thresholds ($T = 1,2,..,100$) were determined and shown in Fig. 3.3. It can be seen that,

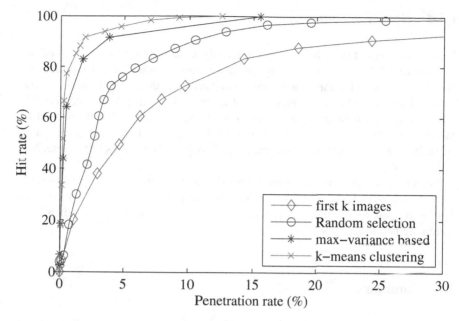

Fig. 3.3 Performance of the system using different selection rules for representative images over PolyU database

at HR=100%, the PR of our method is 12.5 and 15.54% for the k-means approach and max-variance approaches, respectively. In other words, our retrieval algorithms searches only 12.5 and 15.54%, of the database and the genuine image is identified with a probability (i.e., HR) of 100%.

Further, the proposed approaches are compared with Paliwal et al. [3] method and Badrinath et al. [11] method. Paliwal et al. [3] approach is also a match score based method. They used the VA+ file method to store the index codes. This approach chose 171 palmprints for the sample set and achieved an HR of 98.28% only. On the other hand, proposed methods used 130 sample palmprints and achieved 100% HR. Badrinath et al. [11] used SURF features from the palmprints and indexed them using geometric hashing [12]. But, they achieved a PR of 31.89% only [11]. Table 3.4 shows the performance of various approaches.

Table 3.4 PR (%) of the system at maximum HR (%) achieved using different techniques

Approach	HR	PR
Badrinath et al. [11]	100	31.89
Paliwal et al. [3]	98.28	–
Proposed k-means	100	12.5
Proposed Max-variance	100	15.54

3.5.4   Retrieval Time

The retrieval time of the proposed system is analyzed using big-O notation. As shown in Algorithm 3.2, to identify the potential candidates C for a query palmprint q, it is matched against each sample palmprint s_i and it retrieves the $PList$ from the mapped bin and its neighborhood to temporary list L. Note that, this process requires O(k) time as there are k sample palmprints. Note $k \ll N$ where N is the size of the database. In the next step, the P_{id}s that are repeated more times in L are retrieved into candidate set C. Let m be the size of L. This process requires O(m) time. Note that $m \ll N$.

Therefore, the retrieval time of this approach can be approximated as $O(k) + O(m)$ time. On the other hand, a linear search method requires O(N). Thus, we conclude that the proposed algorithm takes less time for retrieval of candidate set than linear search method because $(k + m) < N$.

3.6   Summary

In this chapter, an efficient indexing algorithm for palmprint databases using fixed-length index codes is proposed. We propose an efficient storing method for the biometric database using these index codes such that they are sorted like traditional records and retrieved the best matches similar to the query in a less time. Two different selection approaches are used for choosing the sample palmprints and showed their effectiveness on the performance. The proposed system avoids the sequential scan and use voting to retrieve the best matches. Further, without compromising identification performance, our algorithm performs well than prominent indexing methods. This approach is easy to implement and can be applied to any biometric database.

References

1. T. Maeda, M. Matsushita, and K. Sasakawa. **Characteristics of the Identification Algorithm Using a Matching Score Matrix**. In *ICBA*, pages 330–336, 2004.
2. A. Gyaourova and A. Ross. **Index Codes for Multibiometric Pattern Retrieval**. *IEEE Transactions on Information Forensics and Security*, 7(2):518–529, 2012.
3. A. Paliwal, U. Jayaraman, and P. Gupta. **A score based indexing scheme for palmprint databases**. In *International Conference on Image Processing*, pages 2377–2380, 2010.
4. R. Weber, H.J. Schek, and S. Blott. **A quantitative analysis and performance study for similarity-search methods in high-dimensional spaces**. In *VLDB*, **98**, pages 194–205, 1998.
5. SIFT. **SIFT for matlab:**. http://www.vlfeat.org/vedaldi/code/sift.html.
6. D.G. Lowe. **Distinctive Image Features from Scale-Invariant Keypoints**. *International Journal of Computer Vision*, **60**(2):91–110, 2004.
7. G.S. Badrinath and P. Gupta. **Palmprint Verification using SIFT features**. In *First Workshop on Image Processing Theory, Tools and Applications*, pages 1–8, 2008.

8. Q. ZHAO, W. BU, AND X. WU. **Sift-based image alignment for contactless palmprint verification**. In *2013 International Conference on Biometrics*, pages 1–6, 2013.

9. ILAIAH KAVATI, MUNAGA VNK PRASAD, AND CHAKRAVARTHY BHAGVATI. **A Score-Based Indexing and Retrieval Technique for Biometric Databases**. *International Journal of Pattern Recognition and Artificial Intelligence*, page 1756009, 2016.

10. POLYU. **The PolyU palmprint database:**. http://www.comp.polyu.edu.hk/biometrics

11. G.S. BADRINATH, P. GUPTA, AND H. MEHROTRA. **Score level fusion of voting strategy of geometric hashing and SURF for an efficient palmprint-based identification**. *Journal of real-time image processing*, **8**(3):265–284, 2013.

12. H.J. WOLFSON AND I. RIGOUTSOS. **Geometric Hashing: An Overview**. *IEEE Comput. Sci. Eng.*, **4**(4):10–21, 1997.

Chapter 4
A New Cluster-Based Indexing Technique for Palmprint Databases Using Scores and Decision-Level Fusion

Abstract This chapter proposes a new clustering-based indexing technique for large biometric databases. We compute a fixed-length index code for each biometric image in the database by computing its similarity against a preselected set of sample images. An efficient clustering algorithm is applied on the database and the representative of each cluster is selected for the sample set. Further, the indices of all individuals are stored in an index table. During retrieval, we calculate the similarity between query image and each of the cluster representatives (i.e., query index code) and select the clusters that have similarities to the query image as candidate identities. Further, the candidate identities are also retrieved based on the similarity between index of query image and those of the identities in the index table using voting scheme. Finally, we fuse the candidate identities from clusters as well as index table using decision-level fusion. The technique has been tested on benchmark PolyU palmprint database consisting of 7,752 images and the results show a better performance in terms of response time and search speed compared to the state-of-the-art indexing methods.

Keywords Palmprint · Clustering · Sample images · Match scores · Decision-level fusion

4.1 Introduction

This chapter presents a clustering-based indexing technique using match scores and decision-level fusion. In the literature, there exist few indexing techniques based on match scores which deal with fixed-length codes. The first such attempt is made in [1] for indexing biometric databases. Let m_{ij} be the match score between image i and image j in the database, a match score matrix $M_{N \times N} = \{m_{ij}\}$ is generated by comparing each image in the database with every other image, where N is the number of images in the database. Though the algorithm achieves quicker response time by searching the database based on an evaluation value calculated using the matrix M, the technique takes linear amount of time in worst case. Gyaourova et al. [2] improved the work on match scores by choosing a small set of reference images R from the database. The technique reduces the length of index code from N to R where

© The Author(s) 2017

I. Kavati et al., *Efficient Biometric Indexing and Retrieval Techniques for Large-Scale Systems*, SpringerBriefs in Computer Science, DOI 10.1007/978-3-319-57660-2_4

Enrollment

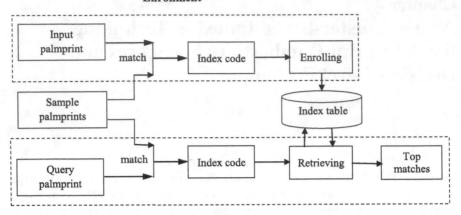

Identification

Fig. 4.1 Overview of the proposed indexing approach

$|R| \ll N$. Similar to [1], for every image in the database, match scores were obtained by matching it against the reference images using a matcher and these sets of match scores act as index code. Further, index code of each individual is stored as a row vector in an index table of size $N \times R$. While identifying a query image, the index code is generated in a similar way and then sequentially searches the index table to retrieve the best matches. This leads to increase of time complexity, i.e., O(N).

Paliwal et al. [3] used vector approximation (VA+) file, which is a space partitioning method to store the match scores. The method uses k-NN search and palmprint texture to retrieve top k similar matches. However, the performance of VA+ file method generally degrades as dimensionality increases. To address these, this chapter proposes an efficient clustering-based indexing technique using match scores. A fixed-length index code for each input image is computed based on match scores. Further, an efficient storage and retrieval mechanism is developed using these indices. An overview of this indexing approach is described in Fig. 4.1. This approach follows these steps: selection of sample images, index code computation, and user enrolment.

4.2   Selection of Sample Images

The selection of sample images from the database plays a crucial role in the performance of the system. Images which are very different from one another and represent the qualities of the entire database should be selected for sample set. In this chapter, we use a clustering algorithm for the selection of sample image set. The database is divided into set of clusters based on their similarity and one palmprint is chosen from each cluster for the sample set. However, in contrast to static clustering approaches like k-means algorithm (which has a serious limitation that the number of clusters k

Fig. 4.2 Selection of sample images

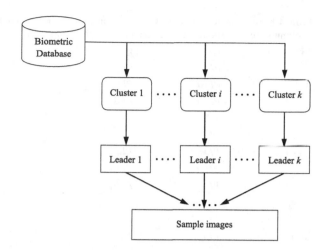

should be fixed before clustering process), we explore an adaptive approach called leader algorithm [4] for partitioning the database.

Leader clustering algorithm makes only a single pass through the database and finds a set of leaders as the cluster representatives (which we call sample images). In this work, we use the match score between the palmprints to determine the cluster similarity. The motivation of using match score as similarity measure is that, usually similar images will have almost same features and so their match score is high, i.e., images in the same cluster will have high match score between them. Leader clustering algorithm uses a user specified similarity threshold and one of the image as the starting leader. At any step, the algorithm assigns the current image to the most similar cluster (leader) or the image itself may get added as a leader if its match score similarity with the current set of leaders does not qualify based on the user specified threshold. Finally, each cluster will have a listing of similar biometric identities and is represented with an image called leader. The found set of leaders acts as sample set of the database (Fig. 4.2). The major advantage of dynamic clustering (such as leader algorithm) is that, new enrollments can be done with a single database scan and without affecting the existing clusters which is useful for clustering and indexing large databases.

4.3 Indexing

This section describes the process of indexing (i.e., enrolling) the palmprints into the index table. The proposed indexing process is similar to the approach described in Chap. 3. This is shown in Table 4.1. The only difference is, this approach uses a dynamic clustering for the selection of samples instead of a static clustering.

Let a be an image and $S = \{s_1, s_2, s_3\}$ be the sample set chosen using the leader clustering. First, we compute the index code of image x by comparing it against the sample set. Note that, the index code consists of k match scores (i.e., keys), each

Table 4.1 Index table consists of $k + 1$ columns, where the first column is the key and remaining k columns are corresponding to one palmprint of the sample set

Score (or Key)	s_1	s_2	–	s_k
0	PList	PList	–	PList
1	PList	PList	–	PList
2	PList	PList	–	PList
–	–	–	–	–
–	–	–	–	–
$x - 1$	PList	PList	–	PList
x	PList	PList	–	PList
$x + 1$	PList	PList	–	PList
–	–	–	–	–
–	–	–	–	–
100	PList	PList	–	PList

against one palmprint of the sample set. Let $x = m(a, s_1)$ be the match score (i.e., index key) of palmprint a against s_1. The proposed approach uses key x to access column 1 of the index table A and enrolls the palmprint identity a in *PList* at bin $A(x, 1)$. This process is repeated with other keys of the palmprint a's index code and its identity is enrolled in the corresponding bin. The other palmprints in the database are enrolled to the index table likewise.

Note that, we have a set of clusters and an index table. The major contribution of this technique is that, the clustering which is used in the proposed approach to select the sample images will produce an additional evidence during identification. This will improve the identification performance of the system.

4.4   Query Identification

This section proposes an efficient retrieval system to identify a query image. Figure 4.3 shows the proposed method of identification. When a query image is presented to the identification system, the technique retrieves the candidate identities from the clusters as well as from the index table which are similar to the query. Finally, the proposed system fuses the candidate identities (evidences) of both strategies to achieve better performance.

Although there are other strategies like multi-biometrics [5–7] (such as multisensor, multi-algorithm, multi-sample, etc.) to retrieve multiple evidences for personal identification, we want to make full use of the intermediate results in the process of computing index code in order to reduce the computational cost. It is easy to see from the Fig. 4.3 that, when computing the index code for a query image to identify the possible matches (Candidate set2) from the index table, we can get set of match scores against cluster leaders. Using them, we can also retrieve the candidate identities (candidate set1) as additional evidence from the selected clusters whose

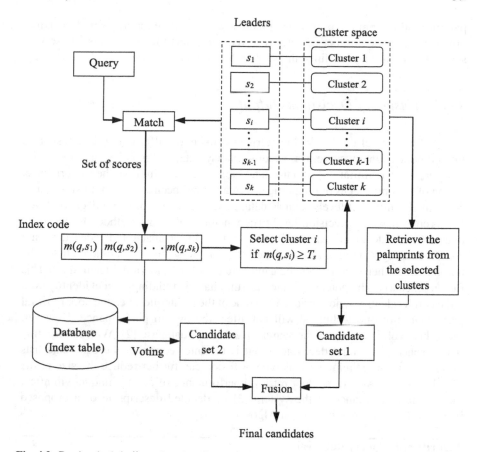

Fig. 4.3 Retrieval of similar palmprints for a query

leaders match score is greater than a threshold. Note clustering has its ability for identification [8].

Let $G = \{g_1, g_2, g_3\}$ be the set of clusters, and $M_q = \{m(q, s_1), m(q, s_2), \ldots, m(q, s_i), \ldots, m(q, s_k)\}$ be the index code of a query palmprint q. Let $x = m(q, s_i)$ be the match score value of q against sample palmprint s_i. The retrieval algorithm uses $m(x, s_i)$ as index to the index table and retrieves all the palmprints found in that bin as similar palmprints to the query into a temporary list. In other words, we retrieve all the palmprints from the index table whose match score value against the sample palmprint is equal to the query. We also retrieve images from the predefined neighborhood of the selected location into the temporary list. Finally, we give a vote to each retrieved palmprint. Further, we also retrieve images from cluster g_i as similar palmprints to the query, if $m(q, s_i) \geq$ similarity threshold. In other words, the clusters whose leader is similar to the query are selected and retrieved that cluster's palmprints into candidate set 1. We repeat this process for each key of the query index code. In our next step, we accumulate and count the number of votes of each palmprint identity in temporary list. Finally, we sort all the identities in descending order based on the number of votes received and select the palmprints whose vote scores higher than a predefined threshold into candidate set 2.

4.4.1 Fusion of Decisions Output

The performance of uni-modal biometric systems may suffer due to issues such as limited population coverage, less accuracy, noisy data, and matcher limitations [9]. To overcome the limitations of uni-modal biometrics and improve the performance, fusion of multiple pieces of biometric information has been proposed. Fusion can be performed at different levels such as data, feature, match score, and decision level. In this chapter, we use decision-level fusion method. With this method, the decisions output (candidate identities) obtained from the cluster space and index table are combined using, (a) union of candidate lists, (b) intersection of candidate lists. The union fusion scheme combines the candidate list of the individual techniques. This fusion scheme has the potential to increase the chance of finding correct identity even if the correct identity is not retrieved by some of the techniques, i.e., the poor retrieval performance of one technique will not affect the overall performance. However, this scheme often increases the search space of the database [2]. With intersection fusion scheme, the final decision output is the intersection of the candidate lists of the individual techniques. This type of fusion can further reduce the size of the search space. However, the poor retrieval performance of one technique will affect the overall performance of the system [2]. A detailed description of a proposed identification technique is given in Algorithm 4.1.

Algorithm 4.1 Query Retrieval

1: **INPUT:** Query palmprint q, Sample image set $S = \{s_1, s_2, .., s_k\}$, Index table: $A(100 \times k)$,
   Clusters $G = \{g_1, g_2, \ldots, g_k\}$, Similarity threshold T_s, Predefined neighborhood λ.
2: **OUTPUT:** Similar palmprints (i.e., candidate set C)
3: **for** each $s_i \in S$ **do**
4:    $x \leftarrow m(q, s_i)$ // $m(q, s_i)$ is the match score (key) of q against s_i

      // Candidate retrieval from G
5:    **if** $x \geq T_s$ **then**
6:       $C_1 \leftarrow C_1 \cup g_i.PList$
7:    **end if**

      // Candidate retrieval from A
8:    **for** $j = x - \lambda$ to $x + \lambda$ **do**
9:       $L \leftarrow L \cup A(j, i).PList$
10:    **end for**
11: **end for**
12: Count the number of occurrences (i.e., $Votes$) of each P_{id} in L
13: Select the P_{id}s in L whose $Votescore$ greater than a predefined threshold T as similar to q and
    retrieve them into C_2.
14: Fuse the candidate sets retrieved from A and G using either Union or Intersection technique

---

4.5 Experimental Results

This section shows the performance of the proposed indexing approach experimentally. The experiments are conducted on PolyU palmprint database to evaluate the performance of the proposed approach. During identification, the proposed approach retrieves a set of candidates from clusters (i.e., candidate set 1) as well as index table (i.e., candidate set 2). Finally, the retrieved candidate sets are fused (Fig. 4.3).

4.5.1 Results

The identification performance using the leader clustering algorithm is evaluated first. Then, the proposed indexing technique performance is evaluated. The variations of *HR* against *PR* at various thresholds of the clustering as well as indexing technique are shown in Fig. 4.4.

The results show that compared to clustering alone, the indexing technique achieves high HR and low PR. The PR of the proposed indexing technique is only 18.7% of the database which is around 30% less than the leader clustering algorithm at 100% HR. The performance using the fusion methods is also compared with the individual clustering and indexing techniques. This is also shown in Fig. 4.4. It can be seen that the combination of clustering and indexing schemes achieves less PR than the individual approaches alone. Table 4.2 shows the performance of the proposed techniques. However, we used the clustering to select the sample palmprints, but it also helps to retrieve an additional evidence during identification. This leads to improved performance of the system. Hence, we can say that, by using intermediate results (i.e., evidence from clusters) the proposed system enhances the identification performance.

Fig. 4.4 Performance of the proposed approach

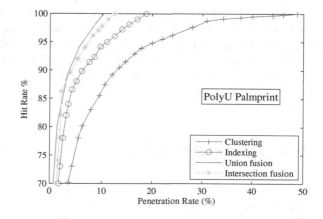

Table 4.2 PR (%) of the system at 100% HR

Approach	PR
Clustering	48.75
Indexing	18.78
Union fusion	10.23
Intersection fusion	12.48

4.5.2 Retrieval Time

We analyze the retrieval time of our algorithm with big-O notation. Let q be the query image, k be the number of sample images chosen, and N be the number of enrolled palmprints in the database. To retrieve the best matches for a query, our algorithm computes the match score of query against the each sample palmprint and retrieves the similar palmprints a. from the index table whose match scores against that sample palmprint are nearer to query, b. as well as from respective cluster of the sample palmprint if its match score is greater than similarity threshold. This process takes $O(1)$ time. However, there are k sample images, so the time complexity this approach is $O(k)$. On the other hand linear search methods require $O(N)$. Thus, our approach takes less time than the linear search approach as $k \ll N$.

4.5.3 Scalability of the System

Nowadays, demands are increasing for the biometric-based personal recognition systems in various applications. Further, most of these biometric systems deal with large-scale databases and their size is increasing at a rapid pace. Hence, scalability of the systems is a huge challenge in these applications. An experiment was conducted to see the scalability performance of the proposed system and is shown in Fig. 4.5. By varying the number of users (100 users, 200 users, 300 users and 386 users), we recorded the *MR* and *PR* at various thresholds. It is observed that, the proposed system performs good for increasing users. In other words, the MR and PR of the system decrease while increasing the number of users which is desirable by an efficient indexing mechanism. This shows the efficacy of the proposed approach for large-scale applications.

4.5.4 Effect of Feature Type on the System Performance

An experiment was conducted to see the effect of the feature type on the indexing performance. This experiment was conducted using two different types of features: (*i*) SIFT and (*ii*) SURF. As seen from Fig. 4.6, the SIFT features, without compromising

Fig. 4.5 Performance of the proposed approach for different number of users

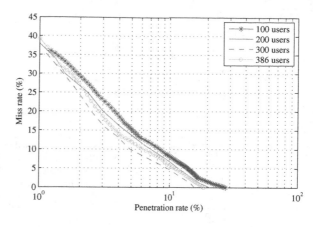

Fig. 4.6 Performance of the proposed indexing approach with different features

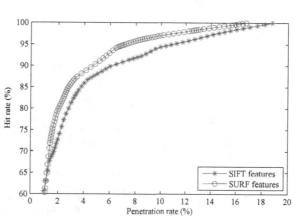

HR, reduce the search space of the system. However, it can be seen that, the SURF features result in slightly higher HR and lower PR compared to SIFT features. This results show that, the feature type also affects the system performance.

4.5.5   Comparison with Multi-biometric Systems

A set of experiments were conducted to assess the performance of the proposed approach against traditional multi-biometric systems. Generally, multi-biometric systems use multiple independent sources (i.e., multiple sensors and/or multiple samples and/or multiple algorithms, etc.) to retrieve multiple evidences for identification. We developed few multi-biometric systems using multiple algorithms for feature extraction, i.e., SIFT and SURF features.

First, clustering was performed using SIFT features and generated a cluster space $CSPACE_1$ and retrieved a set of representatives from it, say R_1. Then, using SURF

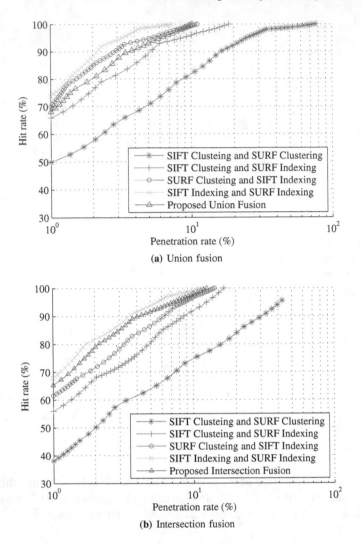

Fig. 4.7 Comparison of the proposed approach with multi-biometric systems

features generated another cluster space $CSPACE_2$ and retrieved representative set R_2. In the next step, using R_1 and R_2, two index spaces were computed $ISPACE_1$ and $ISPACE_2$, respectively. In other words, two different index spaces were computed: one using SIFT features ($ISPACE_1$) and another using SURF features ($ISPACE_2$). These four modules are fused in different combinations to form the following multi-biometric systems:

1. Fusion of SIFT clustering ($CSPACE_1$) and SURF clustering ($CSPACE_2$).
2. Fusion of SIFT clustering ($CSPACE_1$) and SURF indexing $ISPACE_2$.
3. Fusion of SURF clustering $CSPACE_2$ and SIFT indexing $ISPACE_1$.
4. Fusion of SIFT indexing $ISPACE_1$ and SURF indexing $ISPACE_2$.

Table 4.3 PR (%) of the system at maximum HR (%) achieved using different techniques

Approach	HR	PR
Badrinath et al. [10]	100	31.89
Paliwal et al. [3]	98.28	–
Proposed indexing	100	18.78
Proposed union fusion	100	10.23
Proposed intersection fusion	100	12.48

The results of these multi-biometric systems along with the proposed approach are shown in Fig. 4.7. It is observed that, the proposed fusion (union as well as intersection) approaches perform with high HR and low PR than most of the defined multi-biometric systems. However, the combination of SIFT and SURF indexing modules performs well to the proposed approaches with both union and intersection fusion schemes. But, the HR and PR of the proposed fusion approaches are very close to it.

However, note that the defined multi-biometric systems use multiple independent sources (i.e., multiple feature extractors) which require complex processing. On the other hand, the proposed approach used intermediate results instead of independent sources to retrieve multiple evidences and achieved almost similar results. From this we can say that, with less resources and complexity the proposed approach performs well.

4.5.6 Comparison with Other Related Indexing Techniques

The proposed approach is compared with Paliwal et al. [3] method and Badrinath et al. [10] method. Paliwal et al. [3] approach is also a match score based method. They used the VA+ file method to store the index codes. This approach chose 171 palmprints for the sample set and achieved an HR of 98.28% only. On the other hand, proposed methods used 130 sample palmprints and achieved 100% HR. Badrinath et al. [10] used SURF features from the palmprints and indexed them using geometric hashing [11]. But, they achieved a PR of 31.89% only [10]. Table 4.3 shows the performance of various approaches.

4.6 Summary

In this chapter, we propose a new clustering-based indexing technique for identification in large biometric databases. We compute a fixed-length index code for each biometric image using the sample images. Further, we propose an efficient storing and searching method for the biometric database using these index codes. We efficiently used the intermediate results in the process of computing index code that retrieve multiple evidences which improves the identification performance without increasing computational cost. Finally, the results show the efficacy of our approach against state-of-the-art indexing methods. Our technique is easy to implement and can be applied to any large biometric database.

References

1. T. Maeda, M. Matsushita, and K. Sasakawa. **Characteristics of the Identification Algorithm Using a Matching Score Matrix**. In *ICBA*, pages 330–336, 2004.
2. A. Gyaourova and A. Ross. **Index Codes for Multibiometric Pattern Retrieval**. *IEEE Transactions on Information Forensics and Security*, 7(2):518–529, 2012.
3. A. Paliwal, U. Jayaraman, and P. Gupta. **A score based indexing scheme for palmprint databases**. In *International Conference on Image Processing*, pages 2377–2380, 2010.
4. A.K. Jain, M.N. Murty, and P.J. Flynn. **Data clustering: a review**. *ACM computing surveys (CSUR)*, 31(3):264–323, 1999.
5. A. Kumar and S. Shekhar. **Personal identification using multibiometrics rank-level fusion**. *IEEE Transactions on Systems, Man, and Cybernetics, Part C: Applications and Reviews*, 41(5):743–752, 2011.
6. M. Monwar and M.L. Gavrilova. **Multimodal biometric system using rank-level fusion approach**. *IEEE Transactions on Systems, Man, and Cybernetics, Part B: Cybernetics*, 39(4):867–878, 2009.
7. A. Kong, D. Zhang, and M. Kamel. **Palmprint identification using feature-level fusion**. *Pattern Recognition*, 39(3):478–487, 2006.
8. A. Mhatre, S. Chikkerur, and V. Govindaraju. **Indexing biometric databases using pyramid technique**. In *Audio-and Video-Based Biometric Person Authentication*, pages 841–849, 2005.
9. A. Ross, K. Nandakumar, and A.K. Jain. *Handbook of multibiometrics*, 6. Springer, 2006.
10. G.S. Badrinath, P. Gupta, and H. Mehrotra. **Score level fusion of voting strategy of geometric hashing and SURF for an efficient palmprint-based identification**. *Journal of real-time image processing*, 8(3):265–284, 2013.
11. H.J. Wolfson and I. Rigoutsos. **Geometric Hashing: An Overview**. *IEEE Comput. Sci. Eng.*, 4(4):10–21, 1997.

Chapter 5
Conclusions and Future Scope

Abstract This chapter discusses the outcomes of our research. This chapter summarizes our research contributions and also discuss some future research directions.

Keywords Indexing · Contribution · Future scope

The main objective of this research is to explore efficient biometric indexing techniques that can search in reduced space of the database. The outcomes of our research are discussed in Chaps. 2–4 of this book. In this chapter, first we summarize the salient features of the research contributions discussed so far. Finally, we discuss some future directions in this area of research.

5.1 Salient Features of the Contributions

Detailed introduction about the biometric indexing, its challenges are discussed in Chap. 1. A brief discussion about the current developments in the chosen problem is also given. In Chap. 2, an efficient indexing approach is presented using minutiae triplets for biometric databases. Experiments conducted on various fingerprint databases show that this approach enhances the identification performance of the system compared to other triplet-based approaches in the literature. A robust representation for the biometric images is presented by defining a triangulation named extended set, based on the extensions of Delaunay triangulations and triangular hulls. This representation is robust to distortions (mainly in situations like missing or fake minutiae) and minimized the effect of intra-class variations in the system which ultimately increased the HR of the system. Further, like Delaunay triangulation the number of triangles of this new representation (i.e., extended triangulation) is also linear with respect to number of minutiae in the image. Next, the proposed classification over the extended triplets, partitions the database into eight classes. During identification, this limits the search to only particular class of the database leads to decreased PR of the system.

© The Author(s) 2017
I. Kavati et al., *Efficient Biometric Indexing and Retrieval Techniques for Large-Scale Systems*, SpringerBriefs in Computer Science, DOI 10.1007/978-3-319-57660-2_5

A score-based indexing approach is presented in Chap. 3. In contrast to other indexing approaches in the literature, a fixed length index is computed for each image in the database by using a set of sample images. The proposed rules for choosing the samples, efficiently selected the images such that they are different and represent various qualities of the database. Further, an efficient storage structure is developed to arrange the biometric images like traditional database records. This storage structure enabled the retrieval algorithm to perform a quick search during identification. Further, the use of voting (instead of linear search) during identification decreased the number of false matches (i.e., candidate set size). This ultimately decreased the PR and enhanced the performance of the system. Experimental results show that this approach decreases the retrieval time and enhanced the identification performance than other match score based indexing approaches.

An efficient clustering based indexing technique is developed in Chap. 4. An adaptive clustering approach is used for the selection of sample images to make the system suitable for large-scale applications. The system is modeled as a uni-biometric, but extracted multiple evidences for identification like a multi-biometric system by using the intermediate results. This lead to increased performance of the system. The proposed approach makes new enrollments dynamically and without disturbing the existing entries of the system. Though the clustering was used for selection of sample images, it also produces an extra evidence using its intrinsic property of identification. The union fusion technique increased the identification accuracy of the system by combining the evidences from clusters and index table. Further, the intersection fusion is also comparable to union technique and reduces the search space of the system. Finally, the proposed index table for storing the index codes allows us a quick search during identification.

5.2 Future Scope

In this section, we give some future directions for research in our area.

- We experimented the proposed approaches over the databases which are coopera-tive and contain good-quality images. However, the performance of the indexing algorithms depends on the quality of the images. Hence, biometric indexing with the non-cooperative and low-quality images is a challenging problem.
- All of the existing indexing approaches are experimented over the databases which are relatively small. This is due to the unavailability of the large biometric databases for the researchers. Hence, creating and experimenting on such large databases may be another research problem.
- We used k-means and leader clustering approaches for choosing the sample images. Hence, other efficient clustering techniques can be investigated which can further reduce the size of the index code without compromising the indexing performance.

- Securing the biometric data from theft is also another important research topic in the area of biometrics due to the limited availability of the biometric traits. Further, computing the cancelable index codes for biometric identification is also a challenging problem.

Printed in the United States
By Bookmasters